Daphne du Maurier

Twayne's English Authors Series

Kinley E. Roby, Editor
Northeastern University

TEAS 437

DAPHNE DU MAURIER
Photograph courtesy of H&B Graeme, Fowey, England

Daphne du Maurier

By Richard Kelly

University of Tennessee

Twayne Publishers
A Division of G. K. Hall & Co. • Boston

Daphne du Maurier

Richard Kelly

Copyright © 1987 by G.K. Hall & Co.
All Rights Reserved
Published by Twayne Publishers
A Division of G.K. Hall & Co.
70 Lincoln Street
Boston, Massachusetts 02111

Copyediting supervised by Lewis DeSimone
Book production by Marne B. Sultz
Book design by Barbara Anderson

Typeset in 11 pt. Garamond
by P&M Typesetting, Inc., Waterbury, Connecticut

Printed on permanent/durable acid-free paper
and bound in the United States of America

Library of Congress Cataloging in Publication Data

Kelly, Richard Michael, 1937–
   Daphne du Maurier.

   (Twayne's English authors series; TEAS 437)
   Bibliography: p. 150
   Includes index.
   1. Du Maurier, Daphne, Dame, 1907–   —Criticism
and interpretation.   I. Title.   II. Series.
PR6007.U47Z74   1987   823′.912   86-12113
ISBN 0-8057-6931-5

In memory of my mother, Anna Kelly

Contents

About the Author

Richard Kelly holds a B.A. from the City College of New York and an M.A. and Ph.D. from Duke University. His specialty is Victorian humor and poetry. He has written *Douglas Jerrold, Lewis Carroll, George du Maurier, Graham Greene,* and *The Andy Griffith Show,* and edited *The Best of Mr. Punch: The Humorous Writings of Douglas Jerrold.* He has also published recent articles on Lewis Carroll, Robert Browning, and Graham Greene.

Since 1965 he has been a member of the English faculty at the University of Tennessee, Knoxville, where he is now professor of English. His study of the popular "Andy Griffith Show" has received national recognition and has lead to Professor Kelly's appearance on NBC's "Today Show" and on other national television news shows. He is currently writing a critical study of the works of V. S. Naipaul.

Preface

The history of Cornwall is distinct from that of the rest of England. Filled with mystery and superstitions, this small rugged county in southwest England boasts of legendary heroes such as King Arthur, King Mark, and Tristan and Iseult. Cornwall's gothic landscape ranges from tall rocky cliffs that plunge downward into the Atlantic Ocean to wild stretches of moorland. No modern writer has done more to capture the romantic atmosphere and legends of Cornwall than Daphne du Maurier. For over forty years Cornwall has provided her with the background for her most famous novels: *Jamaica Inn, Rebecca, Frenchman's Creek, The King's General, My Cousin Rachel, The House on the Strand,* and *Rule Britannia.* So powerful is du Maurier's obsession with Cornwall and its history that it becomes the real hero of her fiction. Places like Jamaica Inn and Menabilly take on mysterious lives of their own, whispering their ancient secrets to the author, who has spent more than half a century studying and living in these historical houses. The many years she spent living in Menabilly, for example, led to the creation of one of the most famous mansions in all of literature: the sinister Manderley in *Rebecca.*

Daphne du Maurier's Cornwall is now known throughout the world. Her novels and short stories were best-sellers and the motion pictures based upon her tales, such as *Rebecca, Jamaica Inn, My Cousin Rachel, The Birds,* and *Don't Look Now,* have combined to give her an international reputation as the foremost creator of gothic tales of romance and horror.

Despite her enormous popularity—or perhaps because of it—there have been no articles or books written about her. The only body of criticism is the hundreds of book and film reviews that appeared during the past fifty years. The purpose of this study, then, will be to provide the first comprehensive critical and analytical evaluation of her fiction in the hope that it may stimulate further discussion of her works. Her two plays, which are undistinguished, and her biographies of Branwell Bronte and Anthony and Francis Bacon will be her only works not discussed.

The first chapter pieces together what little is known about her life and focuses upon the enormous influence of her famous father upon her development as a writer. The second chapter examines her early novels and traces the dramatic presence of her father in these works. Chapter 3 focuses upon her masterpiece of gothic romance, *Rebecca*. The fourth chapter discusses her development as the foremost writer of romantic fiction, shaping the escapist themes of love, adventure, and rebellion during the turbulent period of the 1940s and 1950s. Chapter 5 analyzes the more introspective novels of the last thirty years, as du Maurier probes the psychological and historical roots of her identity. The sixth chapter surveys and examines her numerous short stories with their emphasis upon the supernatural and the macabre. The last chapter evaluates her character as a writer and her unique contribution to literature and popular culture.

I would like to thank Peggy Morlier and Nancy Strickland, who tracked down the major reviews of du Maurier's novels and the reviews of the films based upon her stories, and who gave me a number of helpful insights into du Maurier's works. I also want to thank the trustees of the John C. Hodges Better English Fund, at the University of Tennessee, for granting me a minisabbatical that helped to complete this study.

Richard Kelly

University of Tennessee, Knoxville

Chronology

1907   Born 13 May in London, the second daughter of actor-manager, Gerald du Maurier.

1916   Family moves to Hampstead; du Maurier attends Miss Tullock's day school in Oak Hill Park.

1917   Begins private lessons at home under the instructorship of Miss Waddell.

1923   Attends finishing school at Camposena, outside of Paris.

1931   *The Loving Spirit.*

1932   Marries Major Frederick A. M. Browning, of the Grenadier Guards, on 19 July; publishes *I'll Never Be Young Again.*

1933   Daughter, Tessa, born on 15 July; publishes *The Progress of Julius.*

1934   Her father, the famous actor-manager, Gerald du Maurier, dies 11 April; publishes *Gerald: A Portrait.*

1936   *Jamaica Inn.*

1937   Starts writing *Rebecca* while living in Alexandria, Egypt, where her husband was temporarily stationed; publishes *The du Mauriers.*

1938   *Rebecca.*

1939   *Jamaica Inn* made into a film, directed by Alfred Hitchcock and starring Charles Laughton and Maureen O'Hara.

1940   *Rebecca* made into a film, directed by Hitchcock and starring Laurence Olivier and Joan Fontaine; wins Best Picture in the Academy Awards; the novel is adapted for the stage; produced in Manchester and London, and five years later in New York.

1941   *Frenchman's Creek.*

1943   Restores and moves into Menabilly; publishes *Hungry Hill.*

1944   *Frenchman's Creek* made into a film, directed by Mitchell Leisen and starring Joan Fontaine, Arturo de Cordova, and Basil Rathbone; *The Years Between,* a play, produced in Manchester.

1945   Publishes *The Years Between;* produced in London.

1946   *The King's General.*

1947   *Hungry Hill* made into a film, starring Jean Simmons, Dan O'Herlihy, and Margaret Lockwood; comes to America to testify in plagiarism trial.

1948   *September Tide* produced in Oxford and London.

1949   Publishes *September Tide* and *The Parasites*.

1951   Publishes *My Cousin Rachel* and *The Young George du Maurier: A Selection of His Letters, 1860–1867.*

1952   Made Fellow, Royal Society of Literature; publishes *The Apple Tree; My Cousin Rachel* made into a film, starring Richard Burton and Olivia de Havilland.

1954   *Mary Anne.*

1957   *The Scapegoat.*

1959   *The Scapegoat* made into a film, starring Alec Guinness and Bette Davis; publishes *The Breaking Point.*

1960   *The Infernal World of Branwell Bronte.*

1962   *Castle Dor,* a novel begun by Arthur Quiller-Couch, which she completed upon his death.

1963   "The Birds" made into a film, directed by Alfred Hitchcock and starring Tippi Hedren and Rod Taylor; publishes *The Glass-Blowers.*

1965   *The Flight of the Falcon;* her husband, Frederick Browning, dies.

1967   *Vanishing Cornwall,* with photographs by her son, Christian; moves out of Menabilly.

1969   Made Dame Commander, Order of the British Empire; publishes *The House on the Strand;* moves into Kilmarth.

1971   *Not After Midnight.*

1972   *Rule Britannia.*

1973   "Don't Look Now" made into a film, directed by Nicolas Roeg and starring Julie Christie and Donald Sutherland.

1975   *Golden Lads.*

1976   *The Winding Stair; Echoes from the Macabre.*

1977   Wins Mystery Writers of America Grand Master Award; publishes *Growing Pains.*

1981   *The Rebecca Notebook and Other Memories* and *The Rendezvous and Other Stories.*

Chapter One
Life and Time
The du Maurier Heritage

Daphne du Maurier has seen to it that her personal life remains shrouded in mystery. There has been no biography written about her, and her own book, *Growing Pains,* presents a very selective and brief account of her early years, up until the time of her marriage in 1932 to Major Frederick Browning. The rest is silence. The standard reference books yield only a few facts, such as the dates of her birth and marriage, the names of her children, and the list of her publications. When I contacted Dame du Maurier to see if she could supply me with some biographical data, I was told that all of her papers and manuscripts are locked away in a London bank "for obvious purposes." Perhaps the papers will be sold at auction some day, and, should they fall into the possession of a university, there is the hope that someone might eventually be able to use them as the basis of a full-length biography. In the meantime, however, her novels, biographies, family histories, occasional interviews, and the autobiography of her early years combine to present a fascinating portrait of this outstanding popular novelist.

Daphne du Maurier is obsessed with the past. She has intensively researched the lives of Francis and Anthony Bacon, the history of Cornwall, the Regency period, and nineteenth-century France and England. Above all, however, she is obsessed with her own family history, which she has chronicled in *Gerald: A Portrait,* the biography of her father; *The du Mauriers,* a study of her family with a special focus upon her famous grandfather, George du Maurier; *The Glass-Blowers,* a novel based upon the lives of her du Maurier ancestors; and *Growing Pains,* an autobiography that ignores nearly fifty years of her life in favor of the joyful and more romantic period of her youth. Daphne du Maurier can best be understood in terms of her remarkable and paradoxical family, the ghosts of which haunt and shape her life and her fiction.

One of the most important figures in the du Maurier family tree is Mary Anne Clarke, the mistress of the duke of York, Prince-Bishop of Osnabruck, second son of King George III. Mary Anne's trafficking in commissions and promotions in the army disgraced the duke's name and finally led to his resignation of the office of commander in chief. Lewd, vulgar, outspoken, fearless, mercenary, manipulative, Mary Anne becomes for du Maurier a symbol of the strong woman whose wit, cunning, and sexuality allow her to compete in a man's world in order to achieve a measure of security for herself and her children.

She leaves a dual legacy to the du Maurier family: fierce determination (embodied in the various heroines of Daphne's fiction) and her pension. In 1809, the year of the scandal, Mrs. Clarke was paid off by the duke with a pension for her life and for her daughter's life after her. Neither her son, George Clarke, nor her daughter, Ellen, mother of George du Maurier, was the child of the duke of York. Nevertheless, Mary Anne's pension saved her daughter's family from starvation and poverty.

In 1831 Ellen Clarke married Louis-Mathurin Busson du Maurier. Louis-Mathurin's father, Robert Mathurin Busson, was a master glassblower who fled to England from his native France in 1789 to avoid a charge of fraud. Financially incompetent but socially ambitious, he created a fictional aristocratic past for himself and added "du Maurier" to his name to bolster his elevated new image. Like his father, Louis-Mathurin was a neer-do-well who attempted the life of an inventor but wound up like Lewis Carroll's White Knight—charming, clever, but hopelessly incompetent. He was scarcely able to provide for his family, though his children loved him and seemed never happier than when he entertained them with his beautiful operatic singing voice. There was always music, if not enough food, in the du Maurier house. Louis-Mathurin and Ellen became dreamers: one day they would become wealthy and famous, and they instilled these fantasies into their children, preparing the way for the rich romantic heritage of George du Maurier's novels, *Peter Ibbetson, Trilby,* and *The Martian.* In addition to sharing his parents' dreams, generated out of poverty and imagination, George grew up believing that his family line went back to twelfth-century France and that his grandfather had owned estates there.

While studying art in Paris, George lost the sight in one eye and abandoned his hope of becoming a painter. Instead, he turned to drawing and before long found himself working for *Punch,* where he developed a distinguished career as a satiric artist. Later in life he tried his hand at fiction and became one of the most popular authors of his day. His three books, with their emphasis upon such contemporary interests as dreams, hypnotism, free association, and automatic writing, helped to reshape the traditional romantic novel. His major interest in the unconscious mind, however, focused upon the idea of a dual personality.[1] As will be seen later, these novels strongly influenced the fiction of his granddaughter, who turned to the writings of Carl Jung to help her explore further the paradoxical nature of the human mind.

In 1873 George's wife, Emma, gave birth to Gerald, her fifth and last child, and the father-to-be of Daphne. The du Mauriers were financially established by this time and moved to a stately house in Hampstead, where Gerald and his brothers and sisters enjoyed an idyllic childhood. In her biography of her father, du Maurier discloses that Gerald was a spoiled, high-spirited child who felt compelled to entertain those around him. At Harrow he became popular with his fellow students by imitating the peculiarities of speech of teachers and students alike. After leaving school he worked for a short time in a shipping office, but found the routine boring and settled for a period of unemployment. During this time he performed in several amateur theatricals, and his success persuaded him to attempt the life of a professional actor. He obtained small roles at the Garrick Theatre, toured in England and America with Forbes-Robertson and Beerbohm Tree, spent a couple of years at the Royalty Theatre with Mrs. Patrick Campbell, and gradually acquired a large following for his innovative, naturalistic style of acting. His first remarkable success came as the hero-crook in *Raffles*. From there he went on to become actor-manager at Wyndham's Theatre. During the fifteen years he spent in management his reputation rose to its greatest height.

Du Maurier's assessment of her father is of special interest, since he became the single most important influence upon her life. Her biography, in a sense, is an attempt, only partially successful, to exorcize this powerful spirit, to distance him, to gain a perspective on him that will allow her the freedom to develop her independence.

She portrays him as an adult Peter Pan who failed to grow up and suffered for it. He never recovered from being the petted youngest child of an enchanting family, even during the height of his acting career. He was constantly haunted by the same moodiness, boredom, and restlessness that, to a lesser degree, George du Maurier had known. There is an extraordinary photograph of him (1911) in *Grow-*

ing Pains sitting in a small kiddy-car, hunched up, looking like an
enormous child wearing his father's clothes.

Du Maurier believes that Mrs. Patrick Campbell turned Gerald
from a boy into a man, but that as an actor he never could achieve
true greatness: "He was not then, and would never be, one of your
true actors. He lacked the intensity, the concentration, the necessary
self-conceit and passionate eagerness of those who talk about their
Work and their Art; and even then he was not known to say, 'Ah!
what I would give to play that part!' "[2] He failed to take himself seriously.

Gerald's chameleon personality and restless spirit become, in his
daughter's eyes, the hallmarks of his individuality. Like the other du
Mauriers, he is a dreamer who will never find satisfaction and fulfillment in this world. When Gerald's sister, Trixie, railed at him
and called him a hopelessly spoiled waster, and blamed their mother
for his upbringing, du Maurier comes to the defense: "Let her try being a man and see what sort of success she would make of it. She
accused him of making a fiasco of his life, just because he was not
settled and smug" (*Gerald,* 93).

Du Maurier writes that "the future and the past were at conflict
within him, and they dragged him different ways. . . . He fell between two periods and was a product of neither." She goes on to
highlight the culture division within him: "He possessed the sentimentality of the one and the cynicism of the other; the moral conventions of the Victorians and the unscrupulous shrug of the twentieth
century; the high standards of the 1880's, and the shallow weaknesses
of 1920" (*Gerald,* 139).

Gerald's paradoxical morality is nicely captured in the following
passage, in which Daphne and her two sisters begin to assert their
sexual liberation:

He was astounded when the child before whom everything was discussed,
and who had met neurotics in the theatre as a matter of course, asked him
whether it was true that boys kissed one another at public schools, and how
very amusing it must be. He gazed at her in horror and had no answer. Men
and women who were not married, but were living together happily in spite
of deserted husbands and wives, came to family lunch on Sunday almost every week of the year, and Gerald was grieved and startled when his own
daughters declared that they did not believe in marriage, and if they ever fell
in love they would prefer to do without the help of the Church, and lead
independent lives. (*Gerald,* 215)

In her autobiography du Maurier openly confesses, "I liked D [her father] better than M [her mother] (which must never be said, even to myself)."[3] Gerald provided a seemingly endless source of excitement and adventure to his three daughters. Writing about herself in the third person, du Maurier recalls the imaginative games she played with her father and his wonderful way of treating them like boys:

> It was fun, too, to play cricket on the lawn with Daphne and Jeanne [her sister], who, in jerseys and knickers, dreamed and thought as boys, calling each other by imaginary surnames and performing tremendous deeds of valour for the sake of a school that did not exist except in their own imagination. Gerald liked teaching them to bowl overarm in orthodox fashion, and to play a straight bat; he bought them boxing gloves and made them tap each other's noses; he discussed *Treasure Island* and *The Count of Monte Cristo,* battles of the Mohicans, and mutinies on ships. (*Gerald,* 189)

Both consciously and unconsciously he made his daughters the center of attention. When they followed in the wake of their famous father to an opening night at the theater, all eyes seemed to turn to them: " 'There she is—look, there are the children—oh, isn't she sweet—look at that one'—and the du Maurier offspring followed their parents along the narrow alleyway that led to the stage door, scarlet with embarrassment, hiding their faces in their party cloaks" (*Gerald,* 221).

After the war, du Maurier began to develop a strong sense of British superiority, with a special distaste for the Americans, a feeling expressed throughout her books. She writes about the "American invasion" of the theater. (Later, in her novel *Rule Britannia* she describes an American military invasion of England.) American actors, actresses, and plays began to take over the British theater, and the managers and businessmen soon joined in the takeover. "It was the dawn of the superlative age and the vogue of the emphasized adjective," she writes (*Gerald,* 208). Words like "darling," "wonderful," "divine," and "marvelous" abounded among the theater set. Du Maurier laments the exportation of American ennui: "There was a sense of desperate expectation in the dreary monotony of nightclubs, a hope that in a new face would come salvation in added excitement; and if the cocktail-shaker produced a pleasant haze it also softened the judgment to a comfortable extent." Even sexuality was reduced to a new low: "People who had hitherto been furtive about sex, and un-

healthily self-conscious, now became brazen and unnecessarily boring"
(*Gerald*, 209).

By 1929 Gerald had no theater, no play, and at age fifty-six he was
thoroughly weary of his profession. Shortly after the death of his
brother Guy in the war, he had almost no male friends. His closest
companions, including his daughters, were all women. Du Maurier
describes this important aspect of her father's character:

From a tiny child Gerald had been spoilt and indulged. Mummie had given
in to him, and Mo [his wife] was Mummie all over again. He had three
daughters and no sons. He was the god and the flame of his little household
of women, and no man in the world could withstand such an onslaught and
remain unspoilt. It spoke well for his inner nature and his true personality
that his character was not objectionable and impossible. . . . Gerald lived
alone amidst his little court of women, having the monopoly of attention in
his small world, without the slightest competition from anyone and with no
interference. (*Gerald*, 230–32).

Du Maurier perceives in her father a "definite feminine strain." He
was "feminine but not effeminate." He possessed "a woman's eager
curiosity about other people's private lives, a woman's tortuous and
roundabout methods of getting to a certain point, a woman's appreciation of gossip, a woman's love of intrigue and drama, a woman's delight and absorption in little mysterious flirtations that last a day"
(*Gerald*, 233–34).

Du Maurier, on the other hand, had powerful yearnings as a youth
to be a boy. "Why wasn't I born a boy?" she complains, "They do
all the brave things" (*GP*, 26). When she was in her young teens she
adopted the persona of a fictitious character she named Eric Avon,
captain of cricket in School House, Rugby. She also conceived of his
two chums, David and Dick Dampier, to be played by her sisters. In
later life du Maurier reflected upon her choice of a male persona: "Yet
why did I pick on Eric Avon as an alter ego, and not an imaginary
Peggy Avon. . . . Whatever the reason, he remained in my unconscious, to emerge in later years— though in quite a different guise—
as the narrator of the five novels I was to write, at long intervals, in
the first person singular, masculine gender" (*GP*, 59). More will be
said about this significant sexual reversal later, but it may be noted
at this point that her relationship with her father and her intuitive
recognition of his feminine strain appear to lie at the heart of her
new-found mask.

As the du Maurier girls grew older they developed an independence that baffled and saddened their father, who could no longer share their confidences: "they stood rooted to their generation, and would not admit him to their world. . . . They were never quite sure of him, never certain of his mood, and they walked away from him, leaving him a lonely, rather hesitating figure" (*Gerald,* 255–56). Du Maurier became increasingly elusive, slipping away to Paris and to Cornwall. Before long she was making money and enjoying her new-found freedom. Gerald once said to her, "I wish I was your brother instead of your father; we'd have such fun" (*Gerald,* 272).

Despite the sparkling moments of joy and adventure shared by du Maurier and her father, the biography finally asserts a sad theme. The changing times, the deaths of his brother and sisters, the maturity of his daughters, and the failure of his own theater management conspire to leave the brilliant actor an unfulfilled man, a person still longing for some mysterious and magical completion to his life. He had long ago abandoned his faith in God. After the death of his brother he became an atheist, like his father before him. As du Maurier observed, "The whole meaning of life boiled down to one thing: affection; being fond of one another. Men and women. Not necessarily being physical, but being companions, swinging hands, yawning in company, eating side by side" (*Gerald,* 285).

Gerald du Maurier died a restless romantic, and he bequeathed to his daughter Daphne the same driving spirit, the same unbounded desires in a frustratingly finite world. As an adolescent du Maurier recorded the following item in her diary: "The old discontent creeps upon me for a while. Vague longings forever unfulfilled" (*GP,* 70). Furthermore, she would have to learn to balance her desire for freedom with her powerful emotional dependence upon her father, a figure who appears wearing many different masks throughout her later fiction.

Like her father, du Maurier learned to play many parts from an early age. She writes, "I saw why D [her father] liked to dress up and pretend to be someone else; I began to do it myself, and so did Angela, and even Baby" (*GP,* 22). Not only could the children enjoy role playing, they also had the benefit of moving to new houses during each summer, new "theaters," so to speak, in which to test their characters. Du Maurier delighted in the freedom she experienced in the country: "we could run outside when we wanted and where we wanted," and these wonderful summers away from Regents Park fixed forever in du Maurier's mind a love for the outdoors and expansive tracts of land. Like the romantic poets, she came to find the city to be a prison, something to flee from.

During these early years she filled her head with tales of adventure, romances, histories, and popular novels, including such books as *Treasure Island, The Snow Queen, The Wreck of the Grosvenor, Old St. Paul's, The Tower of London, Nicholas Nickleby, Mr. Midshipman Easy, Bleak House, Robinson Crusoe, The Mill on the Floss, Dr. Jekyll and Mr. Hyde, The Picture of Dorian Grey, Wuthering Heights,* and *Jane Eyre.* The seeds of her own novels were planted during these intensive, sometimes acted-out, reading sessions. The fascination with the sea, the importance of an historical sense of place, the theme of the dual personality are all reflected in her reading during these formative years.

Her father often took her to the parish churchyard where his family was buried. One such visit finally opened to du Maurier the significance of her family name and the reality of her ancestors: "Then, finally, the trek down to the parish churchyard where Grandpapa was buried, and Big Granny. Aunt Sylvia was in the grave alongside, and there was a memorial to George and another to Uncle Guy, and by this time D would have tears in his eyes, so that one looked away." They would stand there silently, and then Gerald would soon be laughing and joking again and the sadness forgotten. But du Maurier discovered something at the graveyard: "the dead relations in their grave who had never meant very much to me gradually became real and all of them young, while the pictures that Grandpapa had drawn in the pages of *Punch* . . . became suddenly full of meaning" (*GP,* 39).

Du Maurier's growing awareness of the ghosts of her past continued to develop over the years. Although she came to crave isolation, she never felt alone, and when she later came upon the works of Carl Jung, she found his theory of the collective unconscious confirming her own sense of the past being recapitulated in the present. As she observed, "We are none of us isolated in time, but are part of what we were once, and of what we are yet to become, so that these varied personalities merge and become one in creative thought" (*GP,* 65).

She also began to recognize that certain houses possessed unique and mysterious personalities. They embodied the spirits of their ancestors and their histories were as current as their presence. "Who can ever affirm, or deny," she writes, "that the houses which have sheltered us as children, or as adults, and our predecessors too, do not have embedded within their walls, one with the dust and cobwebs, one with the overlay of fresh wallpaper and paint, the imprint of what-has-been, the suffering, the joy?" As she would grow older she would discover one house, Menabilly, and one place, Cornwall, to possess her more than she could ever possess them. "We are all ghosts of yesterday," she continues, "and the phantom of tomorrow awaits us alike in sunshine or in shadow, dimly perceived at times, never entirely lost" (GP, 50).

The du Mauriers maintained a Victorian silence about sexual matters in front of their children. Thus, when du Maurier approached the age of menstruation, she was called aside by her mother and given a peculiar five minute education: "Now that you are twelve, you mustn't be surprised if something not very nice happens to you in a few weeks. . . . All girls, once they have turned twelve, begin to bleed for a few days every month. It can't be stopped. It's just something that happens. And it goes on happening, every month, until they are middle-aged, and then it stops." Upon hearing this sudden revelation, du Maurier stared at her mother, dazed: "To bleed, all my life, until I was old? Was it the same as that illness the poor little Tsarevitch Alexis had before he was murdered in a cellar with his parents and sisters?" (GP, 52). When she asked if her older sister, Angela, also bleeds, her mother replied, "Yes, but I have told her never to talk to you about it, and you must promise me not to tell Jeanne [her younger sister]" (GP, 52).

Du Maurier briefly fantasized that "Perhaps it would never happen. Perhaps I would yet turn into a boy." But it did happen, of course, and she was sent to bed for several days. When Jeanne asked her if she was catching a cold, du Maurier obediently lied: Yes. "So it began," she writes, "the deceit, the subterfuges, of the grown-up world, destroying for ever more the age of innocence" (GP, 53, 54). It was shortly after this traumatic experience that du Maurier created for herself the persona of Eric Avon.

Du Maurier's sexual awakening began in a curious way, during the family's holiday at the shore, with the visit of her thirty-six-year-old cousin Geoffrey, who had divorced his first wife and was staying with the family in the company of his second wife, whom he had recently married. One day at the beach he looked at du Maurier and smiled, and she smiled back. She could not understand why her heart began racing: "I had known cousin Geoffrey all my life, he was fun, he was amusing, D [father] and he were the greatest of friends and companions, for there were only twelve years between them. So why, why, that particular smile?" (GP, 62).

She felt that they shared a secret, an understanding, "and this was something that must not be told to the others." As the family holiday continued, Geoffrey danced with du Maurier, they held hands, but there were no kisses, no whispers. During their last moment together before the family departed for home, Geoffrey took du Maurier for a last look at the sea. As he was telling her how terribly he would miss her, they both noticed Gerald standing up on the cliff looking down at them. "There's Uncle Gerald, spying," he laughed, "we'd better go" (GP, 62, 63).

The forbidden fruit in this case was particularly tempting, not only because it was forbidden but because it involved her father. Du Maurier confesses that she "was reaching out for a relationship that was curiously akin to what I felt for D, but which stirred me more, and was also exciting because I felt it to be wrong" (GP, 64). In this man more than twice her age lies the dangerous and thrilling potential for a kind of imagined, surrogate incest.

Six years later, when she was living by herself at Fowey, Cornwall, Geoffrey visited her again. He was "forty-two years old, as gay and debonair as ever, with the same come-hither look in his blue eyes" (GP, 108–9). "It was like finding a long-lost brother," she writes, "about whom one would always feel more than a little bit incestuous." When du Maurier told him that her father had telephoned from London to see if Geoffrey had been over to see her, "my wicked cousin threw back his head and laughed, the most infectious laugh I have ever known." "We'll pull his leg," Geoffrey said, "when you come back to London, and let him imagine the worst" (GP, 109).

At Christmas Geoffrey visited her again at Ferryside, Cornwall. This time the whole du Maurier family was there. Nevertheless, the forbidden game continued, "with Geoffrey trying to stroke my knees under the table." "Marriage ties," du Maurier writes, "evidently did not worry him, although his wife, Meg, was ill in a nursing home" (GP, 115). After Meg was released from the nursing home and was convalescing in Brighton, Geoffrey made still another visit to Cornwall, and he and du Maurier spent many hours alone together. "The kisses," she remarked, "—never any more than that—continued. . . . The strange thing is it's so like kissing D. There is hardly any difference between them. Perhaps this family is the same as the Borgias.

D is Pope Alexander, Geoffrey is Cesare, and I am Lucretia. A sort of incest" (*GP*, 119). She enjoyed the excitement of creeping downstairs late in her pyjamas, seeing Geoffrey in his pyjamas, and saying goodnight.

Geoffrey finally left for Australia for a year, but before he left Gerald spoke with him about Daphne and informed him that nothing could possibly come of their relationship, despite the fact that Geoffrey announced that he had been in love with her during the past seven years. Du Maurier then records a curious incident that took place at her dentist's office. After noting the striking similarities between her father and Geoffrey, she writes:

Strange, though, that when I was given an anesthetic for the extraction of wisdom teeth at this time—the dentist came up to Cannon Hall to do it— and sudden oblivion descended, I heard someone groaning, "Daddy, Daddy!" through a mist, and it was myself emerging from the darkness. So it was not the Borgia brother but the Borgia father that the unconscious self demanded. (*GP*, 121)

Although she frequently refers to Geoffrey as being "like a brother" and the relationship being a bit incestuous, the experience of waking from the ether may have revealed an incestuous fantasy not easily contemplated when fully conscious. The fact that Geoffrey was married made him an even more perfect object of her erotic feelings, which she transferred from her father to him. Like du Maurier's mother, Geoffrey's wife represented the female who must be displaced.

In her autobiography, du Maurier depicts her mother as a minor character. Du Maurier's life centers upon her father; she is always thinking about him, and later she even writes his biography. Here, on the other hand, is her description of her mother: "She was not an easy person to understand, and both as a child and as a growing adolescent I could never feel quite sure of her, sensing some sort of disapproval in her attitude towards me. Could it be that, totally unconscious of the fact, she resented the ever-growing bond and affection between D and myself?" (*GP*, 67).

In a 1973 essay entitled "The Matinee Idol," du Maurier sympathetically portrays her father as the victim of her mother's intense jealousy and possessiveness. "Twice I saw her really roused, with a high colour and stamping foot," she writes. "The first occasion was when she opened her bill from Fortnum & Mason and saw, in the

middle of a list of items she had ordered, a large case of tea that had
been sent round, on Gerald's instructions, to the apartment of his
current leading lady. Let him order goods on the side if he must, she
told him, but not put them down to his wife."[4]

Her mother's second outburst was more serious. Driving into London in her own small car, she noticed, with astonishment, Gerald's
Sunbeam parked outside a house on the fringe of St. John's Wood.
The house was inhabited by a young actress who had a small part in
one of Gerald's current plays. Mo, as Daphne's mother was called,
drove on to town to shop or visit friends, and on the return trip,
some hours later, she saw that the Sunbeam was still there. "Crisis
threatened," du Maurier writes.

Dinner before theatre that evening was an ordeal. I know, because I was
there. What passed between my father and my mother in the way of accusa-
tion, denial, acknowledgement, contrition, I shall never know, except for
the quick whisper in my ear from Gerald on his way to the theatre,
"Mummy's so angry with me, I don't know what to do." How old was I?
Nineteen, twenty? I don't remember, but I felt then as if he were my
brother, or indeed, my son. The father-daughter relationship had entered a
deeper phrase. (RN, 241)

The fact that du Maurier records these two incidents is interesting
in itself. What is her motivation in revealing that her father probably
committed adultery? Certainly not to judge him or to censure him.
She does neither. Rather, she appears to enjoy a vicarious challenge of
her mother's domination of Gerald and obviously welcomes the new
relationship this establishes between her father and herself. After the
ordeal, Gerald becomes more like her brother (a coequal) or her son
(a dependent). These incidents strengthen the bond between Gerald
and Daphne. Mo, on the other hand, is portrayed as somewhat pee-
vish, stamping her foot, roused to "high colour," and playing the
spy. In du Maurier's reconstruction of the event, her father is the innocent victim and the mother the scolding, intolerant foe of the loving spirit.

This contest between daughter and mother and the quest for an
older and wiser man to serve as both lover and father become obsessive themes in du Maurier's later fiction. The nameless narrator of *Rebecca* vying with Rebecca for Maxim's affection is the most striking
example and will be explored later.

As an adolescent du Maurier enjoyed the privilege of knowing some famous actors other than her father and developed a crush on one lead-ing man: "upon an earlier piece of pink blotting-paper there is the drawing of a heart, pierced by an arrow, and the words 'I love Basil' scribbled upon it" (*GP*, 57). Basil turns out to be none other than Basil Rathbone (of later Sherlock Holmes fame), whom she had seen perform as the hero in the adaptation of her grandfather's novel *Peter Ibbetson*. The dark, handsome actor thrilled du Maurier and her sisters when he later assisted them at their hoopla stall at the annual theatri-cal garden party. Little did du Maurier dream that twenty years later Basil Rathbone would act the part of the wicked Lord Rockingham in the film adaptation of her novel *Frenchman's Creek*.

During her stay in a finishing school at Camposena, outside Paris, in the mid-1920s, du Maurier developed a significant relationship with its director, Fernande Yvon. The school had a firmly established system of ranking the students, and du Maurier wound up in the sec-ond class level, driving her to "cast an envious eye at the elite," the *première* class. And so, she writes, "I set myself a goal. Even if I were not in the *première* I would—by hook or by crook—get myself some-how to the *salon du fond*." The *salon du fond* was the room to which the *directrice*, Mlle Fernande Yvon, would take her favorites after sup-per to play a game known as Truths. With the bravado of her great-great grandmother, du Maurier proceeded one evening, with studied nonchalance and without an invitation, to stroll in to the salon du fond, a book under her arm, *La femme au dix-huitième siècle*, and settled down to read. Expressing astonishment and hostility, the elite group of students fell silent and stared at the bold intruder. "Then," du Maurier writes, "Mlle. Yvon, a glint of laughter behind her eyes, motioned me forward. 'Venez près du feu, mon enfant,' she said. And I knew myself accepted, even welcomed" (*GP*, 74).

"The approval of my idol became necessity," du Maurier recalls, and "I was well and truly hooked" (*GP*, 75). This important role model for the young girl later became one of du Maurier's most de-voted friends, a counsellor, and years later, the tutor of du Maurier's own daughter. She was able to give du Maurier the sense of self-im-portance her mother never could: "Here was an adult, whom I adored, treating me as confidante" (*GP*, 77). When, a few years later, Fernande was dismissed without reason from the school, she and du Maurier spent many days together, traveling, talking. It was to Fer-nande that du Maurier confided her relationship with her cousin Geof-frey, and her mentor advised her to stop seeing him.

It was during the late 1920s that du Maurier began trying her hand at writing short stories, after the style of Katherine Mansfield, but they proved to be disappointing ventures. A relative of hers who worked for Heinemann, the well-known publisher, carried off her stories and a melodramatic play, but the editors found the works unsatisfactory for publication. Meanwhile, du Maurier continued to develop her romantic instincts, which told her she could not survive as a creative spirit if she were imprisoned by a city. Her "desire for roots in the soil" led her to dream: "I would like to go out and live my life in some new colony, where things are just starting, new. Somewhere away from decadence, and modern materialism. Perhaps South Africa, a farm, where there would be no town life, and plenty of riding. I can see myself in my mind's eye, free. Perhaps Fernande could come out and look after me" (GP, 90).

She did not have far to look. Her family, seeking a new summer home, decided to visit Cornwall, and for du Maurier it was love at first sight:

Here was the freedom I desired, long sought-for, not yet known. Freedom to write, to walk, to wander, freedom to climb hills, to pull a boat, to be alone. It could not be mere chance that brought us to the ferry, and the bottom of Bodinnick hill, and so to the board upon the gate beyond that said For Sale. I remembered a line from a forgotten book, where a lover looks for the first time upon his chosen one—"I for this, and this for me." (GP, 97)

The du Maurier family purchased a large, estate-sized house, named Swiss Cottage, built on the water's edge. They renamed it Ferryside, and a team of builders and decorators set to work to have it ready for spring. Located in Bodinnick, Fowey, this house enabled du Maurier to enter the land of her dreams. "I now knew where I wanted to put down roots" (GP, 105), she wrote. Soon she was off exploring the region, enjoying a renewed sense of freedom. The day after her twentieth birthday her family returned to London, leaving her alone at Ferryside. "I was alone, for the first time in my life," she happily noted. "I was free, I could come and go as I pleased, when I pleased, with no parental or even sisterly eye to watch, to make suggestions" (GP, 106). It was during this period that Geoffrey came to visit her. After her exciting escapades with him, she continued to relish the isolation and especially the sea. "I've just realised," she wrote, "that I think of nothing nowadays but fishing, and ships, and the sea, and a seaman's life" (*GP*, 111). The restless, moody sea, stretching away to the horizon towards distant and unknown lands, became for her a powerful symbol of her own spirit. Over the years her obsession with the sea manifested itself time and again in her novels and short stories.

Her Byronic mood grew more intense at Fowey: "It's funny that no one seems really to understand my craving for solitude, that I am sincerely and without posing, happiest when alone. It's my natural state" (*GP*, 116). Nevertheless, her parents seemed eager to see her involved in some socially acceptable enterprise and tried to persuade her to undertake a career in film. An opportunity had arisen whereby she could travel to Budapest in the summer and appear in a film. But she held firm: "No, I would make my own plans. I would spend as much of the summer as I could down at Fowey, by myself, writing stories. Budapest and films were out" (*GP*, 123). And so came to a close a future in films for the remarkably beautiful and photogenic du Maurier. The world she sought to explore lay within the mysterious past of Cornwall and within her family's paradoxical heritage.

Du Maurier developed three obsessions during this time—one with the idea of owning her own boat, another the ancestry of a family named Slade, and still another a mysterious house described to her by her neighbor, Arthur Quiller-Couch. After an arrangement fell through to purchase a boat she wanted, she heard that a man named Ernie Slade, in Polruan, could build her a similar one. She was ecstatic at the news and went to see him. Her conversation with Slade took an interesting turn when he informed her that the old schooner *Jane Slade,* named after his grandmother, was at last to be broken up and that du Maurier could have the figurehead to keep at Ferryside.

While her boat was under construction, du Maurier became more and more intrigued with the history of the Slade family and explored the churchyard at Lanteglos, where the family was buried. "Yes, there it was, the family tombstone," she writes. "Christopher Slade and his wife Jane Symons, died 1885, aged seventy-two. The original of my figurehead, my handsome Jane" (*GP*, 124). The beautiful and mysterious woman whose effigy saw many adventures at sea stamped herself indelibly upon du Maurier's imagination. She could not rest until she knew everything about her and her family, and so, she began to assemble piles of old letters and papers about the family and to draw out a genealogical table of all its members, down to the present day.

"I couldn't get them out of my head," she writes. "Was it fancy, or was it true that Jane dominated them all, even after death." She pushed aside her short stories: "I could think of nothing but Jane Slade, and my own boat that her grandsons had started to build" (*GP*, 125).

The value of her own boat, the *Marie-Louise*, named after her Aunt May, really lay in the fact that she associated it now with the romantic Slade family. "Why did a past that I had never known possess me so completely?" she asked herself, "the people who had built and sailed *Jane Slade* at Polruan, then left her to rot on the beach. . . . Why did I feel so sad thinking of a past I had never known?" (*GP*, 149). She decided that her research into the Slade family finally must be brought to life through a novel. Some lines from a poem by Emily Bronte came to her: "Alas—the countless links are strong / That bind us to our day, / The loving spirit lingers long, / And would not pass away." She decided to name her first book *The Loving Spirit*.

The original Jane Slade would become Janet Coombe, Polruan across the harbor Plyn, and Janet's loving spirit would endure through four generations. In true melodramatic and romantic tradition, du Maurier waited for the right weather to begin the writing: "A terrible wild day, with a howling sou'westerly wind and slashing rain" (*GP*, 151). And thus she began her long career as a novelist.

Du Maurier's second obsession centered upon a house with a history even more intriguing than that of the Slade family. The Quiller-Couches provided her with tantalizing pieces of its past: the woman in blue who looked, so it was said, from a side window, and whose face few had ever seen; the corpse of a cavalier who was found beneath a buttress wall more than a hundred years ago. "And there were the original sixteenth-century builders, merchants, and traders," she recalls, "the Stuart royalists who suffered for their king; the Tory landowners with their white wigs and their broods of children; the Victorian landowners, with their rare plants and shrubs. I saw them all, in my mind's eye, down to the present owner [Dr. Rashleigh, a magistrate], who could not love his home" (*GP*, 128).

Dr. Rashleigh could not love his home, du Maurier reasoned, because he seldom was there. But the house stirred her imagination, and she would visit it at odd times of day and night to contemplate its past. "It was early still," she writes after one visit, "and the house was sleeping. . . . No voices would sound within those darkened rooms. Menabilly would sleep on, like the sleeping beauty of the fairy-tale, until someone should come to wake her." This was truly a haunted house to du Maurier: "She was, or so it seemed to me, bathed in a strange mystery. She held a secret—not one, not two, but many—that she withheld from most people but would give to one who loved her well" (*GP*, 129).

With subsequent visits to the house, du Maurier began to use more possessive language: "there she stood. My house of secrets. My elusive Menabilly" (*GP*, 137). Her love affair with Menabilly, interestingly described as a female, became even more intense than that between du Maurier and Geoffrey, and much more enduring. She would later spend twenty-four years of her life with in its ancient walls and weave several novels out of its history. Most people, of course, best know Menabilly as Manderley, the great home of Maxim de Winter, an imposing and frightening house haunted by the domineering ghost of Rebecca.

Despite her need to be alone with her thoughts and her writing, du Maurier made several excursions into foreign and exotic places where she exhibited a wild and bohemian streak of character. In 1927 she joined a party of select individuals and their host, the millionaire Otto Kahn, in a steam-yachting cruise to the Norwegian fjords. She apparently charmed the young men on the trip, sometimes to the point of spoiling the cruise for the other women. She writes of "scalps dangling from my belt" (*GP*, 144) and of only one male who remained aloof during the adventure, but he, she notes, was absorbed in a book entitled *The Sexual Life of Savages*.

One day, while sitting on the banks of a fjord with Otto Kahn, a man in his sixties, she became the object of his sexual advances. "I wondered how to repel them," she writes, "without seeming ungracious. 'What a glorious day! I must have a swim,' I announced, and, springing to my feet, stripped off my clothes and plunged naked into the water before his astonished eyes. A daring manoeuvre, but it worked." Given his age, Otto did not attempt to follow, and his attentions were more muted afterwards. He later offered to buy her a fur coat at a gift shop, but "This I declined," she writes, "asking for a dagger instead, and the same dagger reposes on my desk today. One never knows when it might come in useful" (*GP*, 143).

Although du Maurier enjoyed these escapades, the writing of her novel occupied most of her time. In the spring of 1930, exactly ten weeks after she began, the book was completed. "I was so excited," she writes, "I could hardly eat my lunch" (*GP*, 159). That afternoon she went over to Lanteglos church to offer thanksgiving and to visit the grave of Jane Slade. Her diary states: "The future faces me with doubt and perplexity. 'No coward soul is mine?' " (GP, 159). While on holiday in France she learned that the respected publisher Heinemann had accepted the book, both for England and America.

While she was waiting for The Loving Spirit to be published she wrote a second novel, I'll Never Be Young Again, in two months time. Soon, everything and everyone around her became grist for her fictional mill. She went on a riding expedition with Foy Quiller-Couch to Bodmin moors and stayed at a wayside hostelry called Jamaica Inn. Here was another building that would possess her imagination. A temperance house in 1930, it had been a coaching stop in the past, "a bar where the little parlour was, the drinking deep and long, fights breaking out, the sound of oaths, men falling" (GP, 164). She would later use this hostelry as the center of her novel Jamaica Inn.

Early in 1931 du Maurier went on a pleasure trip to Paris and discovered the story for her third book: "No ships, no wrecks, no boys running away to sea. The life story of a French Jew—his name would be Julius Lévy. I saw his grandfather, and his mother, and their humble surroundings in Puteaux across the Seine" (GP, 165). Lévy's early life would span the 1870 war between France and Prussia, so du Maurier determined to look up all the history of the siege of Paris and the Fourth of September. "I must work like Fury" (GP, 165), she wrote in her diary.

The Loving Spirit was finally published in February of 1931 and was soon receiving positive reviews, but du Maurier writes that "somehow I couldn't feel excited about it. It belonged to the mood of 1929. . . . It was not mine anymore" (GP, 167). Nevertheless, the novel led to one of the most significant and romantic events in her life.

In the late summer of 1931, a thirty-five-year-old major in the Grenadier Guards, Boy Browning to his fellow officers, second-in-command to the second battalion of his regiment, said to one of his closest friends in the Grenadiers: "I've read a novel called The Loving Spirit, one of the best books I've read for years, and apparently it's all about Fowey in Cornwall. I'm determined to go down there in my boat Ygdrasil, and see the place for myself. Perhaps I'll have the luck to meet the girl who has written it. How about it? Will you come with me?" (GP, 169). John Prescott, the fellow officer, agreed, and they both cruised down the coast to Fowey. Du Maurier's sister Angela spotted them first.

"There's a most attractive man going up and down the harbour in a white motor-boat," Angela said, watching through binoculars. Invited to look through the glasses, du Maurier observed, "H'm, he *is* rather good" (*GP*, 169). The cruising up and down continued for weeks, and local gossip informed du Maurier that the handsome helmsman was called Browning and that he was the youngest major in the British army.

It was not until the following year, 1932, while recovering from an appendectomy, that du Maurier was to hear again about this mysterious visitor who skirted the banks of Fowey. She was one day informed that Major Browning had the *Ygdrasil* laid up in the boatyard in Bodinnick and that he wanted her to go out on his boat with him. The name of his boat, *Ygdrasil,* comes from Norse mythology and means Tree of Fate, a most appropriate name considering how this outing together eventually led to their marriage. "He's the most amazing person to be with," she records in her diary, "no effort at all, and I feel I've known him for years. . . . It was the most extraordinary evening I've ever spent" (*GP*, 170).

Several months later they became engaged and proceeded to introduce themselves to each other's family. Gerald's first reaction to the news of the engagement was to burst into tears and declare, "It isn't fair." But he soon became reconciled to the fact and, because his brother Guy had been a soldier, learned to respect Browning, who had won the Croix de Guerre.

The plan for their marriage was as romantic as their courtship. Early in the morning of 19 July, du Maurier, accompanied by her mother, father, and cousin Geoffrey, set out in the *Cora Ann* towards the church at Lanteglos. Boy Browning and a couple named Hunkins (along to serve as witnesses) followed in the *Ygdrasil.* "All very simple," she writes in her diary, "quickly over" (*GP*, 172). And yet it was not simple at all, for in this quiet pageant she had incorporated love, romance, the history of the Slade family, her cousin Geoffrey, and the final assertion of her independence from her family. "For henceforward," she writes, "I would come to know what it was to love a man who was my husband, not a son, not a brother" (*GP*, 172). For their honeymoon they set forth on another boat, named the *Yggy,* toward the open sea—du Maurier's dream of freedom and adventure and romance all coming together—heading down channel for the Helford River and Frenchman's Creek, the setting of a future novel. As she says, "We couldn't have chosen anything more beautiful" (*GP*, 173). With that sentence Daphne du Maurier draws an end to her autobiography and wraps the next fifty years of her personal life in silence and in mystery.

If du Maurier's courtship and wedding seemed like events taken right out of a romantic novel, then it should come as no surprise that the names of her three children were actually taken from novels. The Brownings' first child, Tessa, was named for Thomas Hardy's *Tess of the D'Urbervilles,* the second child, Flavia, for the heroine of *The Prisoner of Zenda* by Anthony Hope, and the youngest child, Christian, for the hero of John Bunyan's *Pilgrim's Progress.* The family lived a very private life, dividing their time between a small cottage in Hampstead and their house in Fowey, where du Maurier, when she was not writing or attending to her children, went sailing, riding, or walking across the countryside with her sheepdog.

Although eager to settle down in Cornwall for the rest of her life, du Maurier and her family were frequently uprooted as she followed her husband to his various military stations. He always took great pains to see that the various houses they lived in, no matter what country, were arranged as closely as possible to the one they had at home—even to the location of certain pieces of furniture. She describes a typical adjustment to their new surroundings: "So, while desks were placed in new living rooms in identical corners beside new fireplaces, and while he arranged the familiar objects in the right order, I would wander around in a daze, trying to picture the sort of people who had lived in the house before" ("Moving House," *RN,* 279).

But du Maurier's real hold on Cornwall came through her writing. During the next few years she published *The Progress of Julius, Gerald: A Portrait,* and *Jamaica Inn.* While living in Alexandria, Egypt, du Maurier was composing her greatest novel, *Rebecca,* set in Cornwall. "Because I was not happy in the glare of the pseudo East, I shut my eyes and dreamt of Menabilly."[5] Furthermore, the fiction she was to write during the next several decades rarely embodied any of the details of her wide travel during the late 1930s. Her imagination had never left Fowey, where the ghosts of Menabilly left their indelible mark.

The few glimpses we have of du Maurier during the war and after, interestingly enough, come primarily through the pages of women's magazines, not literary journals. *Good Housekeeping, Ladies Home Journal,* and *House and Garden* all ran articles by or about her during the 1940s and 1950s. In an essay entitled "Faces to the Sun," which she wrote for *Good Housekeeping* in 1941, she briefly describes what it was like being with her children during the war, away from her husband. When the threat of enemy air attacks over London became imminent, du Maurier sent her children down to Cornwall to be away from the danger. "But on Tessa's seventh birthday," she writes, "a bomb dropped in the garden next to where the children were playing, and after that they spent most of the time in my mother's shelter." The anxiety that she experienced as a mother of two children, with a third on the way, was intense, but, as the following passage illustrates, she demonstrated considerable courage in the face of adversity:

I was some three hundred miles away from them [her two daughters], and expecting a baby, so it was thought unwise for me to travel. Night after night I used to listen to the news bulletins and hear: "Raiders were again active over the southwest of England," and I knew the children had been in danger again.

When my son was born, a month before Christmas, the raiders were passing overhead night after night on their way to the Midlands. The children were with me again by then, and I used to lie in bed planning our movements should a bomb fall close to us. Their outdoor things were always laid ready on their beds, and I would wrap Christian in his shawl and my own blanket.[6]

The idea behind this article was to encourage the American women, especially those whose husbands were away at war, and du Maurier acknowledges that "the mothers of America will understand what is in my heart as I write." She describes the hardship of seeing her husband leave home just four days after their son is born: "Only a few miles of sea divide him and his men from the enemy on the French coast, and when the nights are foggy and damp and still, I know that he is waiting there, tense, expectant, for the first murmur of invasion—the whine of the dive bomber—and I know, too, with agony and pride, how that strip of coast must be defended, to the last gun, the last man."[7]

Americans who were adjusting to rationing must have found comfort in knowing that the popular author of *Rebecca* was sharing their asceticism: "Somehow, the most primitive things have become a pleasure. The food we eat is a blessing thankfully received, and sleep itself a luxury. Presently the grass will be green again, and once more we shall look out upon the eternal loveliness of spring." Finally, she notes that the war has granted her an unusual education: "The war has brought to me, and to many other mothers, a new sense of understanding, a wish to share trouble and sorrow and suffering, and a determination, too, that when this war ceases, we will never again take things for granted, never again show ingratitude or indifference for the little things of life."[8]

During the war du Maurier's love affair with Menabilly came to a crisis. While she was living with her husband in Kent, du Maurier learned from her sister that everything within Menabilly was up for sale, and "did she want anything?" Her response was immediate: "I wanted her, my house. I wanted every stick of furniture, from the Jacobean oak to the Victorian bamboo." But what was the use, she thought, now that the war had come: "There was no future for man, woman, or child. . . . No, [Menabilly] was just a dream, and would die, as dreams die always."[9]

But in 1943 du Maurier came to Cornwall with her three children and visited the house. She was astonished at what she saw: "No bombs had come her way yet she looked like a blitzed building. The windows were not shuttered now. The panes were broken. She had been left to die." She proceeded to inspect the interior, having crawled through the windows, only to discover moisture everywhere, fungus growing on the ceilings. "I could scarcely see the soul of her for the despair. The mould was in her bones."[10] Convinced that there was little she could do, du Maurier nevertheless phoned her lawyer and asked him to write to the owner of Menabilly to see if he would be willing to lease the place to her for a term of years.

Some days later her lawyer informed her that the owner consented to lease the house, but she was warned that she was crazy to undertake such a lease because there was no lighting, no water, and no heat available. Before long du Maurier started her own battle against the enemy of time, "to live in Menabilly by the time that winter came." She hired architects, electricians, plumbers, and carpenters to put the place back together again, and her fairy tale finally came true: "The house belongs to me."[11]

But as she approached Menabilly, her desire to possess it was tempered by her realization that no one person could ever truly own it: "Slowly, in a dream, I walked towards the house. It's wrong, I think, to love a block of stone like this, as one loves a person. It cannot last.

It cannot endure. Perhaps it is the very insecurity of the love that makes the passion strong. Because she is not mine by right. The house is still entailed, and one day will belong to another." At midnight, when the children were asleep and all was silent, du Maurier sat down at the piano and looked at the panelled walls, "and slowly, softly, with no one there to see, the house whispers her secrets, and the secrets turn to stories, and in strange and eerie fashion we are one, the house and I."[12]

Du Maurier lived in Menabilly from 1943 until 1967, during which time she wrote the majority of her novels and short stories. As her fame grew she became more reclusive and private. Along with her growing reputation as a novelist, a reputation greatly enhanced by Alfred Hitchcock's adaptation for film of *Jamaica Inn* and *Rebecca,* came considerable wealth. Her writings were translated into scores of languages, and she became known world wide. Then the seemingly inevitable happened. Someone else claimed that she had stolen material for her novels.

In 1940 *Rebecca* was translated into Portuguese, and literary critics in Brazil declared that the novel was plagiarized from Carolina Nabuco's *A Sucesora,* published in 1934. Nabuco translated her own novel into English and sent it to a literary agent in the United States. After several years of making unsuccessful rounds at American publishers, the book was sent to an English firm around 1939. The Brazillians believed that the English publisher provided du Maurier with the manuscript so that she could use it as the basis for one of her books. Soon the charge of plagiarism was discussed in the major newspapers of Europe and America. The Brazillian critics claimed that du Maurier stole the plot structure of Nabuco's novel and employed the devices of a portrait of the first wife, of the lining up of the servants on the arrival of the second, of a housekeeper faithful to her old mistress, and hating her new one, and of an old friend of the new wife's husband. What made the charges so damaging was that they could never be settled in a court of law. Miss Nabuco came from so distinguished a Brazillian family that she considered it degrading to sue for plagiarism. Therefore, the battle had to be fought out among critics in the journals and newspapers. The majority of respectable reviewers and literary critics argued on behalf of du Maurier. Harrison Smith in the *Saturday Review of Literature,*[13] for example, argues that *Jane Eyre* is the thematic literary ancestor of both novels, that a first-rate novelist does not have to depend upon her publisher

for plots, and that the similarities between the two works are superficial. After a considerable flurry of articles, letters, and counter letters, the whole affair was forgotten. Or, almost forgotten. When I
advertised in the *New York Times* for material about Daphne du Maurier to use in this book, I received a letter from a Brazillian who told
me that I must not write this study because the author had plagiarized her work from Nabuco.

In 1947 du Maurier was again assaulted with the charge of plagiarism, this time by the son of an American author named Edwina
MacDonald. J. Clifford MacDonald brought a lawsuit against du
Maurier's novel *Rebecca,* her American publisher (Doubleday & Company), and David O. Selznick Productions (which made the film *Rebecca*). The charge was that du Maurier had plagiarized Edwina
MacDonald's stories, especially "I Planned to Murder My Husband"
(a short story) and *Blind Windows* (a novel, published in 1927).

In 1947, du Maurier had to leave Menabilly to come to the United
States to testify at the trial. "I went . . . with Nanny and my two
younger children—I had a boy of six and a half by then, and Tessa,
the eldest daughter, was at boarding school—and once in New York
I stayed with my American publishers, Nelson and Ellen Doubleday.
. . . My only memory of the plagiarism suit was that the notebook
was produced in court, and after cross-questioning the judge dismissed the case" (*RN,* 6). In January 1948, Judge John Bright stated
in his decision: "In reader appeal, in description of scenes and characters, and in literary skill, there can be no claim, in my judgment,
that the latter was copied from the former."[14]

After the trial du Maurier gave the notebook to Ellen as a me-
mento. After Ellen died, the notebook went to her daughter, Puckie,
who returned it to du Maurier. Rereading it for the first time in
thirty years, she decided to publish it in 1980. Perhaps the best thing
to come out of the trial, the notebook sets forth the original outline
and character studies for her novel and provides a fascinating study of
the creative process.

In 1956 a friend of du Maurier's by the name of Beverley Nichols
gave readers a rare glimpse into the famous author's personal life. After visiting du Maurier in Cornwall that year Nichols wrote an interesting article for the *Ladies Home Journal.* As Nichols notes, "this
exceptionally elusive creature" allowed her friend to record some of
the details of the mysterious Menabilly. In the library Nichols discovered some faded snippings from glossy magazines telling of du Maur-

ier's marriage, the birth of her three children, and her occasional presence at functions graced by royalty. There were also paragraphs from newspapers that recorded the astronomical sums earned by her works, "100,000 pounds for this, 50,000 pounds for that."[15]

Some of the details recorded by Nichols capture the essence of du Maurier's character, especially her obsession with her family's history and with the past in general. In one room, for example, she notes some cartoon drawings of Mary Anne Clarke, du Maurier's great-great-grandmother, at her most voluptuous, receiving princes and ministers, who kneel before her, with balloons coming out of their mouths on which are written "the most reprehensible suggestions."[16] The following description of items she found on du Maurier's mantel-piece provides an accurate picture of her eclectic taste and chief interests:

1. A remarkably repulsive china cow with purple udders which was bequeathed to her, unwittingly, by her beloved Gertrude Lawrence.
2. A greatly bemedaled photograph of her husband.
3. A photograph of the head of Demeter. Unframed.
4. A photograph of Botticelli's *Annunciation*. Unframed and mildewed.
5. Four photographs of Sir Gerald du Maurier's aunts. Unframed, mildewed, and curling at the edges.
6. The dialogs of Plato.
7. A crucifix which belonged to her father. Although he was not a Christian, he kissed it every night.
8. A hard, shriveled object that was once a tangerine.
9. A very delicate and sensitive portrait of her grandfather, George du Maurier.
10. Four volumes of the works of Jung.
11. A small empty jar that once held honey from Hymettus.
12. An elementary Greek grammar, purloined from her son Kit when he was at prep school.
13. A sketch of the scandalous great-great-grandmother, Mary Anne Clarke. Unframed, mildewed, curling at the edges and flyblown into the bargain.
14. A casual sketch by George du Maurier of a lady in a crinoline.[17]

There, crowded on the mantelpiece, are the symbols of du Maurier's world: the all-important family tree dating back to Mary Anne Clarke, the striving for roots, both through her own history and through the history of Menabilly itself, the psychologist, Carl Jung, whose works helped her to understand the roots of human behavior through his concept of the collective unconscious, and the philosopher, Plato, whose writings helped shape her thinking about the nature of reason and love.

Nichols asked du Maurier a number of questions that her reading public was eager to have answered. Was the heroine of *My Cousin Rachel* actually a murderer? "I wish I knew," replied the author. "Yes, I created her," she went on to say, "but I don't know if she was a poisoner, and I never shall. . . . You see, when I write in the first person I *become* that person. I literally felt myself becoming Philip when I was writing *My Cousin Rachel* and so I was obsessed with the character of Rachel." She also made some remarks, especially shocking in 1956, about religion. "When I was a little girl," she said, "I was always irritated by the phrase 'God the Father.' It seemed to me grossly unfair. . . . What about 'God the Mother'?"[18]

Were du Maurier in her prime today she would not have been among the ranks of authors who appear regularly on television talk shows to promote their books. As her fame grew through her stories and through the motion pictures based upon them, she became more reclusive. In an essay entitled "My Name in Lights," written in 1958, she writes, "I believe that success and the enjoymnent of it are a very personal and a very private thing, like saying one's prayers or making love" (*RN*, 251). She feels that the outward trappings of success are superficial and embarrassing and spoil achievement. She acquired this feeling through watching her father, the theater idol of his time, pushing his way through a crowd after an opening night: "Adoring, and fiercely proud, I felt instinctively as a small child that the clamor was false, the praise unreal. What the mob really wants is for the artist to fail, so that the whispering campaign can begin" (*RN*, 252). The vanity of it all, the ephemeral nature of fame, means little to du Maurier compared to "the moment when the writer felt the flash [of creativity] and wrote" (*RN*, 254).

The greatest blow dealt to du Maurier came in 1965, when her husband died. The devastating event led her to write some months later a piece entitled "Death and Widowhood." She writes, "We know, and must face it honestly, that life for us can never be the same again. Marriage was not just another love affair, an episode, but the greater half of our existence" ("Death and Widowhood," *RN*, 277). The years ahead she views as a challenge, just as marriage itself was a challenge. In order to ease her pain, she at first took over some of his things for herself. She wore his shirts, sat at his writing desk, used his pens to answer the hundreds of letters of condolence, and by this process came to feel closer to him. The evenings were the hardest to endure: "The ritual of the hot drink, the lumps of sugar for the two dogs, the saying of prayers—his boyhood habit carried on throughout our married life—the goodnight kiss" (*RN*, 274).

Having rejected years earlier a belief in the Christian faith, she found no consolation in the notion of an afterlife. Rather, she asserts: "It is as though every human being born into this world burns, for a brief moment, like a star, and because of it a pinpoint of light shines in the darkness, and so there is glory, so there is life" (*RN*, 274). The spirit of love and of tenderness, she finds, never deserts one, no matter where he or she goes.

Two years later, in 1967, du Maurier moved out of Menabilly. She had rented this manor house on her own, when her husband was at war, and now, alone again she must desert it, as the lease came to its inevitable end. The move entailed not only saying goodbye to the warm family memories spread over two decades, but abandoning the presence of ancient ghosts. Although she moved only a short distance away and lives today in Kilmarth at Par, Cornwall, the move was a richly symbolic one, a leaving behind of a lifetime of memories and centuries of history that all had worked their way into du Maurier's fiction.

Before long, she was happily adjusting to her new home, facing a busy seaport, where she could take long walks with her West Highland terrier, Moray. This house, too, is haunted by ghosts of the past: Roger Kilmarth, who lived in the house in 1327, the Bakers, merchants in the seventeenth century, the Rashleighs, whose descendants owned Menabilly, and "fourteenth-century yeomen, sixteenth-century merchants, eighteenth- and nineteenth-century parsons and squires" ("A Winter's Afternoon, Kilmarth," *RN*, 292). Although still obsessed with Cornwall and its romantic history, she now gives particular notice to a photograph of her husband hanging on the wall of her new house: "beret at the familiar jaunty angle, [he] smiles at me from the dry wall opposite. . . . The smile is infectious, and whether a happy echo from an unforgettable past, or a signal from the Isles of the Blest, it has the required result. Sense of humor returns. I make a long arm and switch off the light, reckoning up the follies of one more useless day, yet knowing in my heart that, but for the absence of the departed skipper, I would not change it for the world" (*RN*, 294).

Chapter Two
The Right Stuff:
The Early Novels

The Loving Spirit

A critic named H. C. Harwood, reviewing Daphne du Maurier's first novel in the *Saturday Review,* writes: *"The Loving Spirit* has the right stuff in it for which a better form may easily be found, by an author obviously possessing and enjoying a love of romantic fiction."[1] Indeed, du Maurier did have the right stuff, the crude materials out of which compelling romantic fantasies are made, and her next two novels, *I'll Never Be Young Again* and *The Progress of Julius,* mark a steady progress in her apprenticeship as a writer. In her fourth novel, *Jamaica Inn,* she finally discovers the proper form for her material and creates one of the classic novels of romantic fiction, second only to her next novel and masterpiece, *Rebecca.*

As was previously noted, *The Loving Spirit* is based upon du Maurier's obsession with the various generations of the Slade family she came to know and study in Cornwall. The novel combines her interest in the past, in Cornwall, in the sea, and in the theme that the power of love transcends one's mortality. The story is set in Plyn, Cornwall. The heroine, Janet Coombe, the source of the loving spirit, is depicted as a female Byronic hero. We first see her standing alone, observing the small world beneath her feet: "Janet Coombe stood on the hill above Plyn, looking down upon the harbour."[2] Du Maurier quickly establishes Janet's romantic, aloof, contemplative, melancholy, and restless nature. "There was a freedom here belonging not to Plyn" (3), she writes.

The novel's central theme is that love must be free to grow despite the shackles that society, with its conventions and codes, threatens to impose upon the individual. The threat to Janet's sense of freedom in this instance is her forthcoming marriage to her cousin Thomas. The duality within du Maurier herself—her desire for adventure and freedom on the one hand, and her longing for love and security on the other—is reflected in her young heroine: "it seemed that there were two sides of her; one that wanted to be the wife of a man, and to care for him and to love him tenderly, and one that asked only to be part of a ship, part of the seas and the sky above, with the glad free ways of a gull" (8). It is as if du Maurier embodies two conflicting characters: her mother's and her father's, the former calling for conventional domesticity and the latter seeking some indefinable ideal. This theme of the double appears many times throughout du Maurier's subsequent novels and becomes a central feature of her romantic fantasies.

After Janet marries she becomes noticeably more quiet and thoughtful as she adapts to her domestic responsibilities. Despite Janet's acceptance of marriage and its attendant confinement, she continues to express strange notions that startle Thomas, as when she tells him that no one in heaven could be at peace knowing that loved ones on earth are in need of them, calling out for their help and their love. She proceeds to make a vow that sets in motion the theme of the novel: "I'll not bide in Heaven, nor rest here in my grave. My spirit will linger with the ones I love—an' when they're sorrowful and feared in themselves, I'll come to them, and God Himself won't keep me" (17).

Meanwhile, Janet gives birth to a son, Samuel, and later to a daughter, Mary. The town folk tell her that she is lucky to have such a fine husband and children, thereby reinforcing her role as mother. Janet's two selves, however, are soon at war again. She enjoys being the contented wife, but the opposing self, "remote, untrammelled, triumphant," asserts itself with renewed vigor. She can find a glimmer of peace only when she is alone, among the wild things in the woods or on the rocks by the water's edge. One day she runs off to be by herself on a cliff overlooking the sea, and she sees a man, his head bowed in his hands, filled with despair and bitterness. This desperate figure is her dream vision of the love that is demanded by fellow creatures and of the love within her that demands to be fulfilled through such needy souls. The figure is also a projection of her other self, the self that demands full spiritual love, a love that is both free and eternal: "she had travelled half a century, out of the world into space, into another time" (29). The figure, finally, is the cry of her future generations for her loving spirit. A believer is precognition, du Maurier employs the idea here through Janet's mystical encounter with her progeny, but in some of her later works she makes more effective and subtle use of the concept.

With the birth of her second son, Joseph, Janet realizes that he is the incarnation of the loving spirit: "he for whom she had been waiting had come at last" (43). She has two more sons, Philip and Herbert, but only Joseph persists in getting his way, embodying the same restless and rebellious spirit as his mother. He becomes Janet's second self, for "he was to do all the things which had been denied her because of her sex" (58). Du Maurier's fantasy to escape from the body of a woman is thus fulfilled in this relationship. Shifting images of one man as a father, brother, son, and lover all come into play at this point. When Joe reaches his teens and decides to go off to sea, there is a melodramatic parting between him and his mother. After he leaves, Janet's craving for his presence seems tantamount to that of a passionate lover: "She curses the weakness of her flesh that hungered for his nearness and his touch, she fought against the demand of her eyes to dwell upon him. To touch his hands and his body that was part of herself, to smell the familiar scent of sea and earth and sun that clung to his clothes, to taste the salt spray that washed from his skin, all these she claimed" (75). The incestuous implications of this passage suggest du Maurier's own reflections about her feelings towards her cousin Geoffrey.[3]

Du Maurier then brings the story in line with the history of the Slade family by having Janet's children, grown older, build a boat in her honor. Her image is carved as the figurehead of the *Janet Coombe*. Janet's divided personality, meanwhile, is reflected in her children: Joe sows his wild oats with the women in Plyn, and the town condemns his evil ways, while his brothers and sisters are praised by the townspeople for their sobriety and responsibility. The *Janet Coombe* finally is completed and the moment it is launched Janet dies, but "her soul passed away into the breathing, living ship" (92).

Du Maurier did not believe in the conventional notion of a Christian heaven. Rather, she saw one's immortality in the collective unconscious, an idea she derived from the writings of Carl Jung and from her obsession with her family history. In an essay entitled "This I Believe," she writes: "There is a faculty amongst the various threads of our inheritance that . . . has not yet been pinpointed by science. I like to call this faculty the sixth sense. It is a sort of seeing, a sort of hearing, something between perception and intuition, an indefinable grasp of things unknown."[4] She goes on to see the power of the unconscious mind to be the salvation of mankind: "If we can communicate, one with another, by thought alone, if a message from the storehouse can act as a panacea to pain, so curing the body's suffering, . . . if dreaming in time can recapture from the past certain events known to our forebears but unperceived by us, then surely a series of possibilities, multitudinous, astonishing, may lie ahead for our children's children" (*RN*, 268). It is this ability to communicate through generations that du Maurier posits within the character of Janet Coombe, and therein lies her immortality, her "loving spirit."

Joseph becomes captain of the new ship, marries a woman named Susan Collins, has three children: Christopher, Albert, and Charles. After Susan dies, he marries a nineteen-year-old girl named Annie Trabb. When Christopher admits to his father that he is afraid of the sea and refuses to take charge of the *Janet Coombe*, Joseph turns the ship over to his nephew, Dick. Later, Christopher decides to go on a voyage with Dick despite his fear, but a report comes back to Joseph that his son deserted ship. Disgusted with his firstborn, Joseph declares that his name never again be mentioned in the house.

The third section of the novel focuses upon Christopher, the third generation of the Coombe family. Married now, he moves with his family back to Plyn and works at the boatyard there. His uncle Philip, the villain of the novel, attempts to bankrupt Christopher by refusing to pay for work he had done at the boatyard. Just as Christopher decides he must kill Philip, a distress call is raised—a ship, the *Janet Coombs*, has broken up. Battling with the other men to save her in the storm, Christopher hears Janet's voice. He tells her to tell his father that he has finally lost his fear of the sea, and with that, he drowns. The men eventually save the ship from the rocks, but a hole is driven into her hull, and she is brought up to rest on the mud, never to sail again. That, of course, is where du Maurier first saw the wreck, a bizarre relic she proceeded to flesh out with this romantic history.

The last section of the book deals with Christopher's daughter, Jennifer, who was only six years old when her father died. With the family boatyard in liquidation, the family moves to London. Jennifer turns out to be a strange child, growing up in a boarding house. She likes to spend time in the men's drawing room, and at school she shocks her friends and teachers by telling them that she not only knows how babies are born but that she has had a few herself.

This imaginative, proud, and outspoken young girl begins to discover the end of innocence when World War I breaks out and she is confronted by military uniforms, fear, anxiety, and the news that her brother Harold has been killed in the war. "The horror of growing up" (278) is upon her, and, like her ancestor, Janet Coombe, she grows restless. After her mother marries a man Jennifer believes to be a fool, Jennifer announces: "I'm going to the place where I belong. . . . I'm going home to my own people—home to Plyn" (294). When she arrives at Plyn she, like du Maurier herself when she discovered Cornwall, experiences a profound sense of her past, her rootedness in this region, and the compelling power of her family heritage. She feels "bound by countless links that none could break, uniting in one another the living presence of a wise and loving spirit" (303).

Jennifer finds that the old boatyard her family used to own has been built up into a thriving industry by a young man named John Stevens, with whom she falls in love. She goes to work for her old uncle Philip, who goes mad and throws all of his legal papers granting his wealth to Jennifer into a fire he sets in the middle of his study. The villain of the novel thus goes up in flames, but John Stevens saves Jennifer from the burning house. The spirit of Janet Coombe, embodied in the figurehead, informed him that Jennifer was in danger and in need of him. Jennifer and John marry, have a son, and after several years of a happy, fruitful marriage, Jennifer, the new embodiment of the loving spirit, observes that there is only one thing in life that matters: "Oh! John, people can say whatever they damn well please about work, ambition, art and beauty—all the funny little things that go to make up life—but nothing, nothing matters in the whole wide world but you and I loving one another, and Bill [their son] kicking his legs in the sun in the garden below" (342).

The psychology of this novel is interesting and paradoxical. On the one hand, it seems to assert that a woman should be free from the encumbrances of domestic life and that she must become like a man in order to realize her potential for adventure. The inner debate over this issue is never clearly resolved in the person of Janet Coombe. She rebels at the notion of becoming a conventional wife, but, at the same time, when her son Joseph is born, she focuses all of her maternal and erotic energies upon him. She acquires a certain kind of freedom after she dies and becomes the spirit within the figurehead that directs the lives of later generations, but this is a far fetched and unconvincing solution to one woman's problems.

Jennifer Coombe, on the other hand, although somewhat unconventional as a child, grows up to be a stereotypical mother. Unlike her ancestors who were possessed by the restless Byronic spirit of Janet, she becomes a happy housewife who insists that the most important thing in life is that she and her husband love one another and share the delightful presence of their baby. This hardly sounds like Janet Coombe, a woman possessed by the mystery and adventure of the sea, who longed always to be by herself with her dreams, who possessed her son and ignored her husband.

The novel is thematically flawed in its confused treatment of the idea of freedom and rebellion. By the end of the book the powerful figure of Janet Coombe is reduced to that of a fire alarm that sends John on a rescue mission. The key to Janet Coombe lies in du Maurier's own chameleonlike personality. Like Janet she harbors the overwhelming need of a teenager to rebel against her parents, to assert her independence, to be alone with her dreams of Cornwall, her dreams of writing books, and her visions of the perfect lover—a composite of paternal, sexual, and filial love.

The autobiographical strain of the novel is always apparent, from its setting to its minor characters. Janet, for example, does not share her sisters' interests any more than du Maurier shared hers. Janet quickly and determinedly goes her own way. In the character of Joseph, du Maurier asserts her own will to be as free and adventurous as a boy, something she always longed to be when she was growing up. Du Maurier reflects her repressed hostility towards her mother, a figure with whom she competed for the love of her father, in her depiction of Christopher's marriage to Annie Trabb. Christopher is also a fantasy figure in another way. He represents the weak male, one afraid of the sea and of manly adventures, who eventually wins his father's approval (a character type that du Maurier later uses in *The King's General,* where Richard's unmanly son finally proves himself a hero). Through the "womanly" passivity and "weakness" of Christopher, du Maurier can deal with the masculine expectations of her father by suddenly and miraculously proving herself in a final moment of crisis, as does Christopher in his attempt to salvage the *Janet Coombe.*

The final persona, that of Jennifer, shows still another side to du Maurier's character, one that insists that the family is the most important unit in society. Writing years later in her essay "This I Believe," she says, "There are certain fundamental laws which have helped to shape us as human beings from the earliest days, and without which we should perish. The strongest of these is the law of the family unit, the binding together of a man and a woman to produce children" (*RN, 266*). She acknowledges that test-tube babies may one day make inroads upon the family structure, but goes on to insist that "In our present state of development we cannot do without the unit. Emotionally, we should be starved. We seek, even in the sexual act, a long-lost comfort. A basic peace, a reunion with ourselves" (*RN, 266*). The fact that marriages often fail is our misfortune, she says, but then she makes this interesting and shocking statement: "Incest being denied us, we must make do with second best. The perfect husband or wife is an illusion, a hero or heroine born of fantasy, something we seldom recognize until, as Hamlet phrased it, the heyday in the blood is tame" (*RN, 266*). Jennifer's marriage to John, like du Maurier's to Boy Browning, can be viewed as the culmination of the autobiographical strain in *The Loving Spirit,* an important and permanent stage of du Maurier's belief in the institution of the family. The shocking notion here, of course, is that she sees an incestuous marriage as an ideal, though forbidden, one. The very fact that she chooses to quote from *Hamlet* adds a certain poignancy to her fascination with incest.

Du Maurier's reflections on women's liberation bear quoting at this point. Set against her views on incest, the following statement seems quite conventional:

Society, as we know it, must disintegrate once the family dissolves. Nothing but the family bond will hold men and women together. Already women, emerging from centuries of submission, fret against their more passive role, demanding equality in all things as their right, but in achieving this they lose their first purpose in life, which is to preserve, to maintain the family. Women have not yet learnt how to serve their families and their own ambitions without conflict, and until they do so husband and children suffer, as well as they themselves. This is the greatest problem of our times. ("This I Believe," *RN,* 266–67)

Throughout her writings du Maurier insists upon the unquestioned value of the family. When Jennifer Coombe dissolves into happiness upon meeting and later marrying John Stevens, du Maurier is not merely establishing a formula for romance novels—though the process of finding a mate is what most romances are all about—but asserting one of her fundamental beliefs about human nature and what she considers to be the most significant instinct of a woman.

When du Maurier published *The Loving Spirit* in 1931, popular romances were not yet in vogue, and the book appeared to be somewhat odd to the reviewers. Geoffrey Terwilliger, writing in the *New York Herald Tribune,* notes the new romantic current in the strong tide of realism:

When some literary historian comes to survey the first third of the twentieth century, he will have fun tracing the roots of the flourishing young romantic revival that is growing up among us. It was in the neighborhood of 1910, if I am not mistaken, that a very earnest wave of realism broke over English fiction, giving it a cold bracing shower of such details as cracked wash basins, animal life under the wallpaper and the like. Life was real, the authors affirmed, and the courageous reader must look not only below the surface but into the cracks. Problems, already well rooted in literary favor, thrived and brought forth the fruit of moral issues. Then the war and in its wake on the one hand a hurt idealism that inverted itself to spare no ghastly detail, but usually hopelessly and helplessly, without the moral favor, and on the other a mad flight into green hats and cocktails ad infinitum, glazing sentimentality with a veneer of so-called sophistication.[5]

Since we now live in an age of mass-marketed romances, such as the Harlequin series, it is important to understand the relative freshness of du Maurier's first novel in the early 1930s, and it is, indeed, with a sense of discovery and pleasure that Terwilliger approaches her novel. "Today's real youngsters," he goes on, "—those still in their twenties—are likely to have a poise and relaxation that make their immediate predecessors seem strained and tense. They are not afraid even of monogamy, in its place." He then makes an astute observation that seems to get at the heart of the modern romance, a feature that makes the genre extraordinarily popular: "Does this mean that a young romanticist has turned her back on what a little while ago we proudly hailed as 'realism?' To me, the answer is no. Certainly to him who has it nothing is more 'real' than a wish, and possibly there is a deeper reality in this view which does not cut out the faith and the ideals than in the kind of realism that was concerned with counting the cracks in the plaster or the buttons missing from a shoe."[6]

Not all of the reviewers were this kind or this perceptive. The *Spectator* sees the work as "gracious" but says that "When Miss du Maurier gains firmer artistic control of her emotions, and ceases to write 'literary' Cornish, her work will be admirable indeed."[7] H. C. Harwood, in the *Saturday Review,* besides acknowledging that du Maurier has "the right stuff," complains that "there is too much death, too much of 'Tisn' the Bible, nor the preacher's words, nor my everlastin' prayers to God that'll save us, Thomas' kind of dialect, too many short cuts to hackneyed pathos, too little that suggests the Coombes are men and women, not rabbits undergoing a Mendelian experiment."[8] All in all, however, the reviews were favorable and predicted a bright future for the young novelist. It would take a few more years for du Maurier to perfect her form, but this first novel had already tapped the deep feelings of her audience and its need for fantasy at a time when escape from reality, especially for women, was intensely sought. Here at last was a woman writing for women, and the sophisticated literary reviews, dominated by men, rarely understood what she was doing.

I'll Never Be Young Again

Du Maurier's second novel, *I'll Never Be Young Again,* is an attempt to communicate the romance of youth and to deal with the question of what is to be done when the romance is over and the romanticism that made it has burned itself out. The story is told in the first person by a young man named Dick and is divided into two parts: "Jake" and "Hesta," reflecting the influences of the two most important people in Dick's life.

The book opens with Dick standing on a bridge in London contemplating suicide. Just as he is about to leap from the bridge, he is grabbed by a stranger named Jake. Jake explains that he was only recently released from prison, having been sentenced for killing a man in a prize fight. He deliberately killed the man because he knew that he had caused an innocent young girl to die by abandoning her after he had enjoyed her sexual favors.

Seven years older than Dick, Jake becomes his best friend, someone to whom he confides his present misery and his future dreams. Jake is a sort of a fairy godfather. He intuits Dick's every mood, understands his thoughts and feelings, and leads him safely through a number of adventures. Sometimes he seems too much of a fantasy figure, especially when he speaks such inflated poetic language as: "But if you listen you'll hear the echo of a lost thing away in the air, like a bird with a song you can't name, high up above you where you can't reach. 'I'll never be young again,' it says, 'I'll never be young again.' "[9]

Dick explains that his father, a famous poet, does not love him and is convinced that he will never make anything of himself. Dick finally rebels by throwing a pile of his pornographic poems before his father and running off toward the bridge, where Jake discovered him in despair. Jake becomes Dick's surrogate father as they go to sea on a Norwegian ship. Over and over, Dick comments on the "assuring comfort" he derives from being in Jake's presence. Although the reader might begin to suspect that a homosexual relationship is developing between the two, a more plausible explanation is that du Maurier, through the persona of the young man she would be, is expressing her desire for an older man suddenly to come into her life, protect her, love and understand her deepest emotions, and take her off to live a life of adventure.

While Dick and Jake are on route to Nantes, their ship wrecks and only Dick survives. He goes to Paris to start a new life with new interests, "forgetting the hell that had been" (170). He is determined not to be lonely and to continue to prove himself and his independence to his father: "It gave me a keen satisfaction, this feeling of intense individualism. The famous father, the outcast son. Being free of him, being a rebel, smashing at authority" (175). We detect here echoes of du Maurier's attempts to stand on her own authority, free from the powerful control of her famous father. This becomes an important theme in her work, one that she develops with great precision and detail in her next novel.

Dick then meets a young bohemian music student named Hesta. He falls in love with her but proceeds to warn her that he thinks the idea of marriage and children is degrading and a routine home life deadly. They decide to live together. After some weeks Hesta protests that she would like them to marry and have a family. All Dick can think of, however, is his dream of becoming a great writer. Having enjoyed her sexuality, Dick finds her presence to be a burden, a responsibility he had not bargained for.

The irony of the novel begins to emerge at this point. Dick decides that he must free himself of Hesta's dominant personality. He begins by breaking down "barriers of individuality and restraint" (264), by making her "enter into submission and so with her own complete surrender she . . . would give me my liberty" until finally she "was there, part of the house, part of my life, part of the general order of things" (265). Without realizing it, he becomes like his despised father who treated his wife in much the same fashion that Dick now treats Hesta. He is also becoming like the young man whom Jake killed for abusing a young girl after he had used her.

Dick goes to London to talk to a publisher about his manuscript. The editor, after reading it, tells him that "you aren't a genius, Richard; you are only an ordinary man" (313) and rejects the book. His dreams smashed, his ideals reduced to practical realities, Dick decides that he wants a secure and settled life in London and asks Hesta to marry him and even to have his child. Hesta, however, has gone to live with another man and informs Dick that she now wants to be a free spirit. Not knowing that his book has been rejected, she tells him that he will forget all about her when his book is published and he becomes famous.

Dick gets the news that his father has died, and he returns to London where he gets a job as a bank clerk. The novel ends with Dick's philosophical observations about the extremes of youth and the peacefulness that comes from having survived those extremes: "I am happier now than I have ever been. The restlessness has gone, the indecision and also the great heights of exultation, the strange depths of desolation. I am secure now, and certain of myself. There is peace and contentment" (343). Finally, of course, he hears in the sound of a singing bird the words imputed to it years earlier by Jake: "I'll never be young again" (344).

Despite the serious flaws in this novel—the poorly conceived narrator, the melodramatic plot, the heavy flights of romantic ecstasy, the bookish dialogue, and the forced conclusion—the book was an important one in du Maurier's development as a writer, and it laid the groundwork for her next novel, *The Progress of Julius*. It is almost as if du Maurier took as a challenge the reviewer's remark that it requires a writer of genius to invest an egotist in fiction with the charm that such a type often possesses.[10] Not only is *The Progress of Julius* a portrait of a volcanic egotist, it is a novel that is in part remarkably shaped by du Maurier's obsession with her father, an obsession that leads to some of her best writing. Even as Gerald du Maurier adopted numerous personae as an actor, he appears in various guises throughout his daughter's novels, but perhaps never so powerfully as he does in *The Progress of Julius*.

The Progress of Julius

Du Maurier's portrait in *I'll Never Be Young Again* of an adolescent egotist, contemplating suicide as a melodramatic gesture of his self-importance, is a shallow one compared to the diabolic, primitive, yet engaging hero of *The Progress of Julius*. Lisle Bell, in the *New York Herald Tribune Review of Books,* notes the paradoxical strain within this work: "This novel is volcanic and elemental, bizarre and brutal. But it is more than that, for underneath its pattern of violence one feels the texture of poetic truth. Julius Lévy becomes the monster he is through logical development of the powers which were his heritage from birth—an endowment of emotions which might have made him a great saint instead of a great sinner."[11]

Julius was born in Puteaux, in 1860, on the banks of the Seine, the son of an Algerian Jew and a crude French peasant girl. His father, Paul, is a quiet, introspective man, who enjoys playing his flute and dreaming. Paul's father-in-law, Grandpère Blançard, on the other hand, is a powerful and lusty individual whose practicality helps hold the family together. Grandpère continually makes fun of his son-in-law's inability to earn his keep, mocks his racial traits, and encourages Julius to join in the attack.

Julius and Grandpère head out one morning in their cart to bargain with peasants for food, and during the trip Grandpère gives Julius some advice that later comes back to haunt him: "That father of yours is a queer fellow now. He sits with his thoughts and his music, he doesn't care for this. You must learn to live with your body, my little one, and laugh and sing, and fill yourself and take everything you want. But don't be a dreamer."[12] Prussian soldiers suddenly appear, and Grandpère is shot and killed while sniping at them, but Julius manages to get back home and warn his family that the invasion of Paris has begun.

During the Lévys' move to safer quarters in Paris, Julius wonders what will happen to his cat. "No—no, my Mimitte, my sweet. I will not leave her for the Prussians" (30), he says, and picks up a stone from the gutter, folds it in a handkerchief, and ties the handkerchief to the neck of the cat: "The animal purred, arching her back, patting the boy's face with her paw. He buried his face in her fur and closed his eyes. Then he ran to the rail of the bridge and threw her over into the Seine" (31). As will be seen later, this bizarre act of possessiveness has far-reaching implications for the future of Julius Lévy.

The Lévys must share a garret with another family, an old woman and her son, a hulking brute of twenty-two named Jacques Tripet, a butcher's apprentice. One afternoon, when Paul is out, Julius discovers his mother in bed with Jacques. He becomes furious at her and reports what he saw to his father. Paul goes into a rage and strangles her in front of his son. Julius could understand why his father had killed his mother: "He didn't want his thing to be spoilt. He would not allow anyone else to have it" (47), and Julius recalled that he had thrown his cat into the river "so that nobody else ever in the world would be able to feed her and stroke her little body. Père had killed Mère for the same reason" (47).

Paul decides that he must flee Paris, and he and the boy hide in a freight car, loaded with stones, heading towards Dijon. Du Maurier's vivid description of this night ride captures the primitive humanity of the father as he attempts to shield his son against the pain of the journey:

Paul Lévy felt for him in the darkness, he stretched out his arms and found him. He drew off the wet clothes and put Julius close to him upon his own naked body, underneath his clothes, next to his skin, so that his own warmth should go to him and their flesh would be together; he held him tight in his arms that Julius should feel only his body and not the jolting stones, while he himself lay on his back, shaken and bleeding, his head against a great jagged-edged stone. And Julius slept. (56–57)

Graham Greene, who had recently published *Stamboul Train,* in reviewing du Maurier's book in the *Spectator,* singles out the episode cited in the quotation above for especial praise: "Her description of the night journey from Paris through the German lines, of the child Julius and his father hidden in a goods-wagon, touches the imagination with her selection of sounds and movements, the shunted trucks, the whistle of the steam, the foreign voices coming up the rails."[13]

Having reached safety, Paul decides to return to Algeria, the place of his birth, only to die shortly after his arrival. Julius, meanwhile, dedicates his time to selling goods and swindling people in the marketplace. Although he is living with a Rabbin, he tells him that "I was not meant to sing in the Temple. This is my thing, selling to make a profit. Something for nothing, something for nothing" (65). And with that, Julius lays the foundation for his future.

He soon grows bored in Algeria, believing that he could develop his fortune better in London, and so he goes to the house of Martin Fletcher, an English pastor living nearby, in order to learn the English language. Like his father, who kept him alive during their journey from Paris and was later quickly put out of mind by Julius, the Rabbin and Fletcher, after they fill Julius's needs, are similarly cast aside and forgotten. The only person who mattered to Julius at this time was a fourteen-year-old whore named Elsa: "She made him feel important; she was willing and eager to please" (95).

On his way to London, Julius discovers that Elsa is also aboard ship, and she tells him that she cannot bear to be without him. Reluctantly, he lives with her in London while he starts working for small pay in Grundy's bakery. He throws all of his energy and skill into his work and before long acquires enough patronage and control to be able to demand that Grundy sell the shop to him. His vengeance upon his poverty and his dream of future power combine to make him into a frightening figure:

To Julius Lévy, there was ecstasy in this secret life of his; the knowledge that he could not fail was like a hidden jewel worn against the skin, to be touched and caressed in the darkness with warm sensuous fingers; nor would he share the brilliance of the secret with anyone in the world. These English people were pawns in the game. (112)

Employing innovative business practices and catering to the slightest whims of his clients, Julius eventually expands the bakery into a cafe and then into a chain of cafes. Part of his success is achieved on the backs of his underpaid employees, including Elsa, who works for no pay until, finally, she dies of a hemorrhage. Julius, of course, not seeing nor caring that he helped to kill her, continues with his plans to ring all of England with his restaurants. He finds that he can "create and control [life] as he wished, and this world was his own world for his own purpose" (151). All of his business deals turn out successful, and he soon finds himself a millionaire.

Julius marries a woman named Rachel Dreyfus, and they have a child named Gabriel. She becomes the turning point in Julius's life: "He saw her, in his mind, as a business proposition, she was another of his cafes, raw as yet and undeveloped, but when the time came she would be as he wanted her" (198). As the years pass and success follows success, Julius reaches his fiftieth birthday and takes time to reflect. He is bored with his success, becomes restless, and wants to live even more intensely than he has up to this point. He discovers an all-consuming object to which he can devote the remainder of his life. He looks at his beautiful young daughter and "a fierce sharp joy came to him stronger than any known sensation, something primitive like the lick of a flame and the first taste of blood" (225). He recognizes in her "a sudden secret adventure, tremendously personal to them both, intimate in the same absorbing fashion as a disease is intimate, belonging to no one else in heaven and earth, egotistical and supremely self-obsessing" (229).

He proceeds to spoil her, pushing the child forward before her time, indulging her every wish and encouraging her every craze. It is at this point in the novel that du Maurier begins to shape her two major characters after her father and herself and to temper the ego-maniacal strain of Julius with a certain engaging human feeling. Like du Maurier's own mother, who is pushed into the background of her autobiography and who is depicted as jealous of the intimacy between her husband and daughter, Rachel is quickly displaced by Gabriel in Julius's attention: "Rachel had to watch them, both so dissimilar physically and yet like to each other in blatant intimate fashion: the same laugh, the same brilliance, the same swift understanding and appreciation; and one was her husband and one was her child. . . . They were exactly alike in their supreme blind egotism" (232).

The theme of incest explored in *Growing Pains* also finds its way into this novel. While listening to Gabriel playing the flute, Julius is reminded of his father, only the song his father played opened up visions of a spiritual city, whereas Gabriel's song disclosed "another whisper and another city . . . one that opened and gave itself up to him; there were eyes that welcomed and hands that beckoned, all mingled in extravagant confusion of colour and scent and ecstasy" (242). Her song stirs erotic longings in Julius for his own daughter and leaves within him "a sensation in mind and body that was shame-ful and unclean" (242). He complains to her, "But you don't let me get at the core of you, do you?" (242). She then takes his hands into hers and tells him that they are "the best things about you" and then drops them and moves away. "There you are," he says, "that's what I meant. Are you a child or do you do it on purpose?"

Meanwhile Julius continues to encourage Gabriel's various crazes— the flute, hunting, racing, and yachting. Rachel accuses her husband of spoiling her, and they argue, after which he turns to Gabriel to ask what is wrong with Rachel. "Gabriel laughed softly and reached for a cigarette. 'Jealous,' she said" (247). The competition between daughter and mother for the love and attention of Julius is quickly settled, however, when Julius decides that Rachel is getting fat and that "her utility was over now." "Gabriel would make as good a host-ess when she came out next year," Julius thinks. Furthermore, "She was modern, too, in advance of her age" (249).

Gabriel resents her mother's presence at Melton, where the family goes to relax: "Mother brought her disapproving personality and stifled the house in an atmosphere of gloom" (250). And so, it delights Gabriel to learn that Rachel develops a pain in her side that takes her back home, leaving her alone with Julius and her friends. Du Maurier's language in describing Julius at this point is reminiscent of her description of Gerald: "he was always so enthusiastic, so terribly alive. He had a personality that stood out above everybody else's; he made other men—young men especially—look so stupid, so callow and inexperienced. Papa was young, too, but in a different way. Subtle, queer, there was a glamour about him" (255). When du Maurier wrote these words, her father was old, tired, and about to die, but his vital and dominant presence continued to preoccupy her.

The pain in Rachel's side turns out to be cancer, and she later commits suicide, freeing Gabriel from her gloomy spirit and her strong claims upon Julius. Julius plans an elegant, wild party to show off his daughter and to possess her more completely: "Papa . . . invented this night for her as though it was his wish to make her drunk for the first time" (260). Like a demonic force, "he was cruel, he was relentless, he was like some oppressive, suffocating power that stifled her and could not be warded off" (261). The submerged sexuality in this episode suggests that Julius would once and for all possess the mind and body of his daughter, that her individuality must be destroyed, consumed by his own passion.

Like du Maurier herself, however, Gabriel asserts her independence and refuses to allow her father to dominate her: "she would be the victor, she would never be possessed. . . . She would keep him by her side and draw upon his strength; his life was her life, his flesh and blood were her flesh and blood, but it would never be he who was master" (263). These are very significant words, for they mark du Maurier's declaration of independence, an independence that would become fiercer as time went on. She would proceed to develop powerful female characters whose inner strength and independence set them apart from other women of their time. The heroine of her next novel, for example, develops precisely out of this critical psychological turning point in du Maurier's relationship with her father.

After Rachel's death, however, Julius and Gabriel manage to work out a happy relationship, traveling, enjoying new sights and sensations together. "Gabriel was the ideal companion," du Maurier writes, "the other self. . . . They understood one another. They were happy together" (271). During the war years, 1914–18, they temporarily drift apart—Gabriel working in hospital wards, driving lorries, nursing the wounded—and Julius, selling "Lévy's Bully Beef" and boots to the military. He comes out of the war the wealthiest man in England.

With the war ended, Julius becomes bored, enters politics, buys and reforms several newspapers, but Gabriel once again becomes his true obsession. He begins spying on her and questions her about her relationship with other men. He asks if she is sleeping with these men and refuses to accept her denial. After one such heated exchange, Gabriel announces that she is tired and is going to bed, and then there is this curious dialogue:

> "Gabriel," he said. "Gabriel. . . ."
> She glanced at him over her shoulder and shook her head.
> "No," she said.
> He gazed at her sullenly, gnawing at his finger-nails, hating her. (288)

The unspoken words here seem to be a plea for a sexual encounter, one that will allow Julius to possess his daughter more completely than he has been able to up to now—thus his crazy jealousy of her and his sudden violent hatred at her rejection of his plea. All of Julius's ambitions and all of his power finally focus upon the sexual act. He must have Gabriel, and if he cannot have her completely then no one will have her at all.

One day he and Gabriel sail to an isolated strip of land where the sea ran deep. Gabriel announces that she is going to bathe and undresses in front of Julius, an act that recalls du Maurier's own bizarre striptease before the millionaire Otto Kahn in Norway. Naked, she stretches her arms up into the air and tells her father: "I'm not going to be me anymore. I'm going to be somebody else, Gabriel will go forever." Tired of being a free spirit, she has decided to settle down with another man: "I'll be domesticated and subservient and humble" (298). She then wades out into the deep water. Julius follows after her and commits the ultimate act of possession:

He was on her before she could move, seizing her throat in his right hand, bending her legs with his knees, pressing her down into the water beneath him. She fought in his grip, but was unable to free herself. . . . He went on holding her beneath the water, beating her legs with his knees, and he wondered how long it would be before her body sagged under him, and grew limp, and was lost to him. (299)

As if engaged in a mad incestuous rape, Julius consumes his own creation. Like the cat he drowned to save from the Prussians and like his mother, whom his father murdered for sleeping with another man, Gabriel is destroyed so that no other man might ever enjoy her.

The final chapter of the novel simply recounts the last twelve empty years of Julius's life. He goes to live in Paris, the place where he was born. He is "finished—burnt out," and his monstrous ambitions for power and sexual domination are parodically reduced to an extravagant desire for food. He grows old and fat, becomes a recluse within his palatial home, and soon grows paranoid, suspecting that everyone is out to cheat him. The thought of Gabriel never enters his mind. A hollow man in a wasteland of wealth, he falls victim to a stroke at age seventy-two and some days later dies peacefully, never really understanding the meaning of his life.

Although many reviewers praised this novel, most of them failed to understand it. Case in point: Elmer Davis, writing in the *Saturday Review of Literature,* complains that the plot is "schematic as a fugue," that Julius Lévy is "only a Balzac exercise on a single trait," and that "Julius Lévy himself is no more credible than Elmer Gantry."[14] Davis seems to ignore du Maurier's interesting fusion of Julius's tenacious avarice, his lust for power, his sadism, and his sexual fixation upon his daughter. He likewise overlooks the manner in which du Maurier designs Julius's conquest of the macrocosm as an ironic contrast to his pathetic failure to possess the more intense and elusive microcosm, represented by his daughter. The character of Julius Lévy captures an essential truth about human nature, and he is certainly no less believable than someone like Howard Hughes who, in his later years, lived like Lévy, a paranoid recluse, given to far more bizarre practices and thoughts than du Maurier's fictional creation. The important point, however, is that the significance of Julius Lévy does not derive simply from his believability but from his power as an archetypal figure, an incubus, who would possess the entire world through the sexual devouring of his daughter. His addiction to lavish food in his last years serves as an ironic comment on hunger for sexual domination. Lurking in the background of this novel is the figure of the mysterious Jew, Svengali, and his sexual domination of the beautiful young Trilby, in du Maurier's grandfather's novel, *Trilby.* Byron's Manfred and Shelley's Cenci, with their quest for omnipotence and sexual domination (and obsession with incest), are also prototypes for du Maurier's hero. Julius is like a demonic god who sacrifices his only begotten daughter, not on behalf of others, but on behalf of his own volcanic egotism. He is the creator whose ultimate creative act is one of annihilation.

The antecedents of Julius's madness must not be forgotten. Like Graham Greene's great villain Pinkie Brown in *Brighton Rock,* a demonic thug who once hoped to be a priest, Julius once longed to be a Rabbi. The mixture of Jewish mysticism and peasant sensuality makes him an interestingly paradoxical character. His intensity and fanatical dedication to an idea could well have made him into a great saint, but there is nothing in du Maurier's own heritage—given her father's and her own agnosticism—to allow her to depict Julius's spiritual development. Nevertheless, she does show Julius to be a great dreamer despite all of his material wealth. His is a dream of power and sexual dominion.

Several reviewers were shocked and disgusted by some of the events in the novel. Anne Armstrong, in the *Saturday Review,*[15] was repelled by the scenes in which the ten-year-old Julius discovers his mother in bed with another man and coldly watches his father strangle his mother. A writer for *Punch* wonders why du Maurier has given us "materialism at its ugliest" and hopes that she will use her remarkable gifts on "something more attractive."[16] Yet, none of the critics noticed, or, if they did, decided it better not to mention, the rather shocking suggestions of incest in this novel. (Similarly, they made no mention of the erotic feelings of Janet Coombe for her son Joseph in *The Loving Spirit.*)

Graham Greene's review of the book is especially notable in light of his hero in *Stamboul Train*—a Jewish businessman interested only in profit, who manipulates people to advance his own career. Greene says that du Maurier's book "is saved by its energy. This is not life, but it is sometimes a very good stage adaptation of life. The characters murder, fornicate, kill themselves with admirable vigor." On the negative side, he feels that her prose is "bookish," that she lacks "literary tact," and that she "is a romantic masquerading as a realist."[17] He is probably correct on all three counts, though this novel is far less "bookish" than her previous two. Greene himself, however, is a romantic masquerading as a realist, and there is nothing wrong with that. With her subsequent novels, du Maurier openly becomes a writer of romantic fiction, having paid her homage to Balzac, Zola, and Hemingway. Through the relationship of Julius Lévy and Gabriel she has set forth a profound truth about the female imagination and discovered the powerful fantasy character of the assertive, independent woman, one who would risk death to be free to find the consummate lover.

Jamaica Inn

The figure of the strong, assertive, independent woman glimpsed in *The Progress of Julius* comes into full bloom in *Jamaica Inn*. This haunting tale, set in the Bodmin moor around the year 1835, is the story of twenty-three-year-old Mary Yellan. The novel opens with Mary being driven in a coach to Jamaica Inn, reflecting on her recent past. While nursing her mother through a long illness, Mary began to acquire a sense of independence. She knew that at her mother's death her only recourse would be to leave the pastoral Helford countryside and go to live with her Aunt Patience and Uncle Joshua, who run Jamaica Inn. Mary wrote to her aunt and was told that she was welcome to come provided she attend bar at the inn. Upon her mother's death, Mary set out for her new home.

Du Maurier's description of Mary's journey to Jamaica Inn establishes the rich gothic tone of the entire book. The landscape moves from the remembered, peaceful, rolling green hills of Helford to the grim, cold, and isolated moors. "The country was alien to her," and the shining waters and green hills of Helford were now remote and "hidden perhaps forever."[18] The lashing, pitiless rain stings the windows of the coach and soaks into "a hard and barren soil." There are no trees here except for one or two that have been "bent and twisted from centuries of storm" (9). "It was a scrubby land, without hedgerow or meadows; a country of stones, black heather, and stunted broom" (10). Du Maurier invests the landscape with a character as vivid as any of the people in the story: "No human being could live in this wasted country, thought Mary, and remain like other people; the very children would be born twisted, like the blackened shrubs of broom, bent by the force of a wind that never ceased, blow as it would from east and west, from north and south. Their minds would be twisted, too, their thoughts evil, dwelling as they must amidst marshland and granite, harsh heather and crumbling stone" (21).

When she arrives at the inn she is met at the door by her uncle, Joss Merlyn. He is described in terms of massive strength and size, clearly bigger than life: "He was a great husk of a man, nearly seven feet high. . . . His frame was so big that in a sense his head was dwarfed, and sunk between his shoulders, giving that half-stooping impression of a giant gorilla, with his black eyebrows and his mat of hair" (24). His last name conjures up the Cornish legends of Merlin and dark magic, while his wife's name, Patience, testifies to her superhuman endurance under the domination of this man. Remembered by Mary's mother as bright and vivacious, Patience is now a broken woman, her "face fallen away . . . and her eyes large and staring, as though they asked perpetually a question" (26). Life with Joss has caused her to become a beaten woman, fearful, passive, nervous, and paranoid. She knows the secrets of Jamaica Inn, and they have nearly destroyed her.

Du Maurier bifurcates the demon-lover father of *The Progress of Julius* into two characters for this novel. Joss embodies pure malignancy, while his younger brother, Jem, is a handsome, arrogant, mysterious man who, by the end of the story, becomes Mary's lover. While each character is psychologically less interesting than Julius Lévy and more one-dimensional, such a division resolves du Maurier's ambiguous attitude towards her father: she can hate and prevail over his dominance by battling Joss and yet express her erotic feelings and her need for security to Jem. A reviewer for the *Times Literary Supplement* noted the duality in saying that "Mary found herself a kind of Jane Eyre with two Rochesters."[19] Such bifurcation is common in fairy tales, where there is an evil witch and a fairy godmother, discrete embodiments of a mother's changing and confusing personality that can be more readily understood and dealt with by a child.

Although written in the third person, practically all of the events of the story are filtered through the thoughts and feelings of Mary Yellan, who gradually uncovers the mystery of Jamaica Inn. Late at night she secretly watches a group of frightening-looking men arrive with wagons to store their hidden cargo in the locked room of the inn. She hears mysterious footsteps overhead, suggesting a stranger whose presence is unknown even to Joss and his evil crowd. Mary quickly comes to realize that Joss and company are smugglers, men who will not stop at murder, and whose bounty is transported from the coast up to Jamaica Inn.

One day Mary attempts to follow Joss and gets lost among the moors. Francis Davey, the vicar of Altarnun, happens by on horseback and rescues her. She confides in him all of her anxieties, and he tells her that, should she ever be in trouble, she can depend upon him to help her. But the strange, transparent eyes of the albino minister make her uneasy, and she turns to Jem Merlyn for comfort. At first she is reluctant to express her affection for this proud and mysterious figure because he is related to the villainous Joss, but she soon falls in love and rides into Launceston with him on Christmas Eve where he plans to sell some of his stolen horses.

Before she leaves, however, Joss, in the midst of one of his five-day drunken bouts, tells Mary the secrets of his trade. He and his men are "wreckers," that is, they set up false lights along the coast to cause ships to crash into the rocks. They then gather up the booty from the shipwreck and from the drowned and murdered passengers and crew. He confesses that he has killed people with his bare hands, stoned them, and remained untroubled until he drinks and sees their dead faces in his dreams.

After Mary and Jem arrive in Launceston, Jem suddenly vanishes in the Christmas crowds, and Mary is left to find her way back to the inn. Again she is picked up by Vicar Davey. Despite his protestations of help, Mary senses Davey to be a malignant force, a mutant: "his physical departure from normality was a barrier between him and the rest of the world. In the animal kingdom a freak was a thing of abhorrence, at once hunted and destroyed" (196). Still, she confides in him the secrets of Jamaica Inn, to which he replies that the government is prepared to put an end to these false coastal lights by beginning to patrol the shore.

When Mary returns home she finds her uncle drunk and his men gathered for a trip to the coast. They force Mary to accompany them on their brutal enterprise. Harry the pedlar, one of the most grotesque members of the crew, attempts to fondle Mary and attacks her when she resists, but she manages to escape from him to a high hill from which she watches the men at work, ripping rings off of dead hands, picking corpses clean of any valuables, robbing haphazardly, each man for himself. Back at the inn, Joss tells Mary that she is now a party to their adventures as much as Patience, and there can be no escape for either of them: "we have enemies on either side of us now. We have the law on one hand, and on the other" (230). And with that a new mystery is introduced: who else is after them? Joss then waits downstairs with a gun across his knee in preparation for a visitor.

Mary subsequently makes several attempts to obtain help from the vicar and the magistrate, Mr. Bassat, and to tell them that Joss plans to escape. Not finding them at home, she returns to the inn and discovers that Joss has been stabbed in the back. Bassat and his men, meanwhile, arrive, search the house, and find that Patience has also been murdered and that Harry the pedlar has been locked up in the room where the booty used to be kept. Mary begins to suspect Jem of the double murders. Davey then arrives on the scene, and he takes Mary back with him to his house.

Alone with Davey, Mary begins to suspect that he is a madman. In one of his drawers he has a picture he drew of his congregation with sheepheads instead of human heads and the preacher with a wolf-head. He explains to Mary that "I am a freak in nature and a freak in time. I do not belong here, and I was born with a grudge against the age, and a grudge against mankind. The silence is gone, even on the hills. I thought to find it in the Christian Church, but the dogma sickened me, and the whole foundation is built upon a fairy-tale. Christ himself is a figurehead, a puppet thing created by man himself" (319). Furthermore, Joss Merlyn also turns out to have been a figurehead, manipulated by Davey, the mastermind behind the "wreckers." It is Davey who committed the double murders to prevent Joss from accusing him to the police. Like the Druids of old, Davey delights in associating himself with the ancient, pagan times when "the rivers and the sea were one, and the old gods walked the hills" (319). Davey forces Mary to cross the moors with him. Soon they hear a band of men led by Jem, who shoots and kills Davey.

Having heroically survived the hardship of this pagan, twisted wasteland with its cold and brutal inhabitants, Mary looks eagerly towards her return to the peace of Helford. As she heads towards her old home, however, she meets Jem Merlyn on the road, and he offers to marry her. Mary willingly accepts the proposal, knowing they will face rugged times together but assured that their love will make a new life tolerable.

This is du Maurier's first novel to contain the main features of the gothic romance: the isolated, bleak landscape; a house filled with mystery and terror; violence and murders; mysterious strangers; villains larger than life; and a strong-minded woman who bravely withstands a series of challenges and who is rewarded with marriage and the promise of a full life. Du Maurier obviously drew heavily upon *Wuthering Heights* and *Jane Eyre* for some details of her novel, especially in her descriptions of the atmosphere and the characters of Joss and Jem Merlyn, who bear some of the traits of Heathcliff and Rochester. The most original character in the book is Francis Davey, a fascinating throwback to pre-Christian Cornwall.

One of the most interesting and positive reviews of *Jamaica Inn* was written by Sean O'Faolain, who places the author on the same level with Robert Louis Stevenson:

Jamaica Inn [makes] one realise how high the standard of entertainment has become in the modern novel. I do not believe R. L. S. would have been ashamed to have written *Jamaica Inn*, with its smugglers, wreckers, wild moors, storms, its sinister inn, misplaced confidences, pretty and gallant heroine, and romantic love story. Joss Merlyn, the inn-keeper, is in the good old tradition of Simon Legree *cum* Long John Silver, and his brow-beaten wife has had many prototypes in similar fiction. . . . There is here all the melodrama that one can desire—and let nobody say "It is an old fashion." The old fashion was good.[20]

Du Maurier's reputation as a novelist was further enhanced when Alfred Hitchcock turned *Jamaica Inn* into a motion picture, starring Charles Laughton as Sir Humphrey Pengallan (a character not in the novel), Leslie Banks as Joss Merlyn, Marie Ney as his wife, Maureen O'Hara as Mary, and Emlyn Williams as Harry the pedlar. Making his last English film and first costume piece, Hitchcock felt that he was pressured into directing this film, a work that he never freely undertook and one that he regretted later. He is quoted as saying, "I am primarily interested in the Jekyll-Hyde mentality of the squire."[21] Fascinated by dual personalities, du Maurier does not develop this theme in the novel but merely allows us to glimpse Joss's more human character. Her actual psychological strategy is to create two separate personalities—Joss and Jem—rather than to dwell on the duality of one character. Later, in *The Scapegoat*, she explores the theme of the double in great detail. Hitchcock imposes his own reading of the book upon the motion picture.

One aspect of the novel that the film successfully captures is the image of Joss Merlyn as a father figure, dominating the orphaned Mary. Raymond Durgnat, in his essay "The Strange Case of Alfred Hitchcock—Part Six: Touch and Go," observes that after the Squire (Laughton) tells Mary that she has no one to depend on but him, "she yields to him as a child abandons herself to be led, decidedly, head bowed, gag obscured by her cloak's hood, through a bustling crowd, in a bondage which is more than physical, which is worthy of *L'His-*

toire d'O, and which is by far the most romantically expressed emotion in the film."[22] The excuse Mary offers in the novel for remaining at Jamaica Inn is that she must help her Aunt Patience, but a more cogent psychological reason is that she possesses a masochistic as well as a rebellious strain. Lacking a father, she seeks both domination and love and finds the former in Joss and the latter in Jem.

If du Maurier did not enjoy Hitchcock's version of *Jamaica Inn,* she must have found justice done to her novel in the recent film version made for television. Produced by Peter Graham Scott and directed by Lawrence Gordon Clark, the film was aired in the United States in June of 1985. Jane Seymour appears as Mary, Billie Whitelaw as Patience, Patrick McGoohan as Joss, Trevor Eve as Jem, and John McEnery as Davey. Derek Marlowe's screenplay is very faithful to the novel, and the location scenes in Cornwall capture the rugged and desolate atmosphere of du Maurier's descriptive passages. Despite the excellent casting—the characters look as if they walked right out of the novel—the artful photography, and the fidelity to the novel, the picture seems too long and moves at too slow a pace. All of the characters and all of the melodramatic action are there, but the film lacks a center of consciousness and the emotional intensity needed to engage the audience's imagination and to pull the picture together. The performances are highly professional and polished to the point where we marvel at the acting instead of believing in the emotions. The scenes between Mary and the Reverend Davey, however, are compelling ones. John McEnery's calm, deliberate, almost musical speech, combined with his cadaverous appearance, make him a remarkably sinister villain.

Du Maurier's first four novels proved to be interesting in and of themselves and to provide her with character types, buildings, and atmosphere that could be transformed and developed in her masterpiece, *Rebecca.* The power of the dead Janet Coombe to haunt the present, the incestuous theme of love between father and daughter, the egotism of Dick and Julius, the submissiveness of Mary Yellan, the mysterious and evil Jamaica Inn, the sinister Vicar Davey are all resurrected in new and vital forms for du Maurier's next novel, one of the most remarkable and popular books of the twentieth century.

Chapter Three
Rebecca

During the late eighteenth and early nineteenth century a new genre, the gothic romance, flourished in England. Writers such as Horace Walpole (*The Castle of Otranto,* 1764), Mrs. Anne Radcliffe (*The Mysteries of Udolpho,* 1794), and Matthew Gregory Lewis (*The Monk,* 1796) touched the reading public's subconscious fears and terrors through their bold accounts of seductive villains and houses of horror and mystery, set against a pseudo medieval atmosphere of castles, cliffs, lonely moors, and storms. After the gothic vogue faded, according to Kay Mussell, "romances were dominated by domestic dramas that defined and defended the female virtues of 'purity, piety, domesticity, and submissiveness' for a wide audience of women." During and after the popularity of domestic romances, Mussell observes, "the tale of gothic adventure continued in the work of such writers as Mrs. E. D. E. N. Southworth, whose heroines faced dangerous dilemmas and behaved with spunk and aggressiveness."[1]

The most skillful use of gothic details, however, appeared in Charlotte Bronte's *Jane Eyre* and Emily Bronte's *Wuthering Heights,* both published in 1847. While borrowing such gothic details as the lonely house, the ferocious Byronic gentleman, the mysterious glimpses that are later explained as resulting from the imprisonment of that gentleman's insane wife in the attic, the horrible death of the maniac in the burning mansion, and the indomitable power of love, Charlotte Bronte breathes new life into the genre and makes the story eminently believable. Similarly, Emily Bronte's inhuman specimen of gothic violence—the brooding, melancholy Heathcliff—the stormy atmosphere, bleak landscape, and the passionate love story are drawn from the conventions of the gothic romance but raise the form to a higher imaginative pitch. After the achievements of these two belated masterpieces of romanticism, the novel slowly moved towards an emphasis upon realism, a tide that Robert Louis Stevenson, at the end of the century, attempted to stem with his tales of adventure and his sharp criticism of authors who sought to "compete with life" in their fiction. The gothic romance, in any event, was for all practical purposes a dead form until Daphne du Maurier revitalized it in 1938.

Du Maurier's *Rebecca* is the first major gothic romance in the twentieth century and perhaps the finest written to this day. It contains most of the trappings of the typical gothic romance: a mysterious and haunted mansion, violence, murder, a sinister villain, sexual passion, a spectacular fire, brooding landscapes, and a version of the mad woman in the attic. Du Maurier's novel, however, is much more than a simple thriller or mystery. It is a profound and fascinating study of an obsessive personality, of sexual dominance, of human identity, and of the liberation of the hidden self. The real power of the novel, as will be seen, derives from du Maurier's obsession with her father and her resolution of that obsession through the fantasy structure of her novel.

As several reviewers have noted, the novel is a sophisticated version of the Cinderella story. A young girl, not long out of school, poor and dependent upon the whims of a vulgar old social climber who is staying at Monte Carlo, meets a mysterious and unhappy widower of forty, Maxim de Winter, who is obsessed with a secret from his past. He is an aristocrat, the owner of Manderley, one of the finest country houses in the south of England. The two marry and return to Manderley, where the nameless, naive heroine discovers that she is overshadowed by the perfections of Rebecca, Maxim's first wife. The macabre housekeeper, Mrs. Danvers, is dedicated to protecting the memory of Rebecca from the innocent new mistress of the house. The second Mrs. de Winter, however, discovers that her jealousy of Rebecca is mistaken when she learns that her husband hated his first wife and is brooding over the fact that he murdered her and is now threatened with blackmail by Rebecca's wicked cousin, Favell. A last-minute discovery, however, frees Maxim of any sense of guilt. He is declared innocent at a trial; Mrs. Danvers burns down the house; and Maxim and his wife are free to start their lives anew.

The novel opens with the haunting sentence, "I dreamt I went to Manderley again."[2] By making the naive, nameless second Mrs. de Winter the narrator du Maurier is able to develop and sustain the mystery plot while she explores the central question of identity. The narrator appears, at first, to have no true identity, having been the toady to the gross Mrs. Van Hopper (a typical expression of du Maurier's snobbish anti-Americanism), only to fall under the powerful shadow of Rebecca herself. Du Maurier describes her as devastatingly plain, "with straight bobbed hair and youthful, unpowdered face, dressed in an ill-fitting coat and skirt and a jumper of [her] own creation" (9).

Maxim de Winter, by way of contrast, is described as "arresting, sensitive, medieval in some strange inexplicable way" (15). The narrator associates him with the medieval past "where men walked cloaked at night, and stood in the shadows of old doorways, a past of narrow stairways and dim dungeons, a past of whispers in the dark, of shimmering rapier blades, of silent, exquisite courtesy" (15). This language reflects the narrator's indomitable romanticism, her love of chivalry, mystery, and ancient history. Given the fact that her own life up to this point has been stiflingly dull, she is prone to romantic fantasy, and Maxim de Winter is the perfect star of her gothic melodrama. She later describes him as someone who did not seem to belong to the bright landscape; rather he appeared more like a Byronic hero, "standing on the steps of a gaunt cathedral, his cloak flung back, while a beggar at his feet scrambled for gold coins" (38). This passage foreshadows her subsequent comparison of herself to a dog at his feet, revealing her total subservience to her gothic hero.

Forty-two years old, Maxim is precisely twice the age of the narrator. His mysterious past fascinates the young girl. He seems possessed by the spirit of Rebecca as we see him standing on a tall cliff, "within six feet of death" (29), looking down towards the sea. The more he refuses to discuss his past, the more the narrator (and the reader) wants to know about it. Rebecca, the real hero of this novel, is dead, but her presence marks every turn of thought of the living characters. The narrator is struck by Rebecca's inscription in a book she had given Maxim: "Max was her choice, the word was her possession, she had written it with so great a confidence on the fly-leaf of the book. That bold, slanting hand, stabbing the white paper, the symbol of herself, so certain, so assured" (43). She is all the things the narrator is not. She is the demon that must be exorcized from both Maxim's and the narrator's minds.

Later the narrator cuts this fly-leaf from the book and sets it on fire: "The flame had a lovely light, staining the paper, curling the edges, making the slanting writing impossible to distinguish. The fragments fluttered to grey ashes. The letter R was the last to go, it twisted in the flame, it curled outwards for a moment, becoming larger than ever. Then it crumpled too; the flame destroyed it" (57). This symbolic murder of Rebecca anticipates the conclusion of the novel when Manderley, the embodiment of Rebecca, burns to the ground, freeing Maxim and the narrator once and for all of her dominance.

While a few reviewers remarked upon and found distasteful the narrator's snobbishness and insidious inferiority complex, they failed to note her suppressed sexuality. This timid, mouse of a creature, as the reviewers call her, uses revealing language in recording her first approach to Manderley. As Maxim drives her up the road to his estate, she is overwhelmed by the beauty of the azaleas and shrubs and describes the road and fauna with words and phrases like "serpent," "penetrate," "throbbing," "penetrating even deeper," "blood-red," and "slaughterous red" (64–65). The narrator's sexual rival, of course, is Rebecca. Convinced that Maxim is consumed with grief and love for his dead wife, the narrator must face the dragons that protect Rebecca's memory.

The major dragon is the housekeeper, Mrs. Danvers, a figure dressed in black and associated with death. The narrator's first meeting with the servants proves to be traumatic: "Someone advanced from the sea of faces, someone tall and gaunt, dressed in deep black, whose prominent cheek-bones and great, hollow eyes gave her a skull's face, parchment white, set on a skeleton's frame" (67). Mrs. Danver's hand is described as "limp and heavy, deathly cold, and it lay in mine like a lifeless thing," and her voice is also "as cold and lifeless as her hand had been" (67). She is the evil witch, the embodiment of Rebecca, who must be destroyed before the fairy tale can be concluded. Like Rebecca herself, Mrs. Danvers represents a powerful hold on Maxim that recreates the oedipal love triangle in du Maurier's own life. In the fantasy structure of this novel, du Maurier neatly resolves her own desires by having Maxim suddenly reveal that he never loved Rebecca—in fact, he hated her—thereby making the narrator the only woman he ever loved. The wish fulfillment expressed in that surprising turn of events is of paramount importance to the success of the novel, for it touches deeply the psychological need some daughters have to believe that their fathers love them more than anyone else, especially more than their mothers. It seems that du Maurier was never totally convinced of her father's all-consuming love for her—her mother, with prior claims upon him, not to mention the various actresses in his company upon whom he showered gifts and attention, were rivals for his affection—and so, through this adult fairy tale, she transforms her father into Maxim de Winter, a man seemingly dedicated to the memory of his domineering wife, who suddenly reveals that he loves none other than the nameless adoring heroine who, if she were named, might be called Daphne.

Du Maurier has taken the Cinderella story a step further than the account in folklore. Indeed, the nameless heroine of her novel has been saved from a life of drudgery and marries a handsome, wealthy aristocrat, but, unlike the prince in "Cinderella," Maxim is old enough to be the narrator's father. In fact, as will be seen later, du Maurier strongly suggests Maxim's paternal character. Like Cinderella, du Maurier's heroine is an orphan, performing menial tasks for the foolish and uncaring Mrs. Van Hopper. Instead of having a fairy godmother, the young girl has simply the good luck of meeting Maxim de Winter in Monte Carlo. In only a matter of days they fall in love, and Maxim frees the down-trodden girl from Mrs. Van Hopper by proposing to marry her and carry her off to his mansion. In many fairy tales and in most romances, marriage is the essential ingredient that rewards the heroine and provides the all-important climax to the story. In *Rebecca,* on the other hand, the marriage comes early in the story and is merely the prelude to the fierce competition the heroine faces in winning the love of her husband. Du Maurier takes the evil stepmother and the beautiful sisters of Cinderella, so to speak, and introduces them later on in the persons of Mrs. Danvers and Rebecca. At the fancy ball at Manderley, again reminiscent of "Cinderella," the heroine is tricked into dressing like Rebecca, an act that leads to her miserable humiliation. It is not simply marriage, then, that brings du Maurier's heroine happiness, but the symbolic death of Mrs. Danvers, the destruction of Manderley, and the exorcism of Rebecca, thereby crowning her with her true and unique title of Mrs. de Winter (no longer the second Mrs. de Winter) and assuring her that she is the solitary recipient of Maxim's love and devotion.

Du Maurier's fascination with the sea is brought to bear in a significant way upon this novel. The sea is associated with Rebecca's death by drowning (although, as we find out later, she was dead before her boat sunk). Thus the narrator becomes uncomfortable in its presence, for it represents the pain of her husband, the mystery of his past, and the violent terrors of the unknown. When she first comes to Manderley, Mrs. Danvers informs her that Rebecca's room in the west wing overlooks the lawn running down towards the sea. Since this room has been kept intact since Rebecca's death, the narrator must live in the east wing. She says, "I was glad our rooms were in the east wing and I could lean out my window and look down upon the rose-garden. . . . I could not hear the restless sea, and because I could not hear it my thoughts would be peaceful too. . . . I began to dread any mention of the sea, for the sea might lead to boats, to accidents, to drowning" (119, 120).

The narrator finds peace and comfort in the rose garden and in the idyllic, landscaped place called Happy Valley, where the flowers are white and gold and graceful, in contrast not only to the sea but to the violent colors of the shrubs along the driveway to Manderley. Happy Valley, however, proves to be an illusory garden of Eden, for down beneath it lies Rebecca's boathouse, a place harboring sinister and sexual secrets that tempt the narrator to pry. The theme of forbidden knowledge is central to the novel. The narrator thinks, "Somewhere, at the back of my mind, there was a frightened furtive seed of curiosity that grew slowly and stealthily, for all my denial of it, and I knew all the doubt and anxiety of the child who had been told, 'these things are not discussed, they are forbidden' " (202). To make things even worse, Maxim tells her that he married her for her innocence and that there is some knowledge, forbidden to her, that he never wants to see reflected in her face.

The narrator proceeds to ask Frank Crawley, Maxim's agent, about Rebecca. He informs her that Rebecca drowned in a boating accident and that Maxim identified the body, which was washed ashore two months later, some forty miles up the channel. Rebecca's boat is called *Je Reviens,* meaning "I come back," a prophetic name, for not only does Rebecca come back to haunt the present but at the end of the novel the boat itself is discovered by a diver who provides evidence that it may have been deliberately scuttled. Continuing to fill in details of the past, Frank says that Rebecca "was the most beautiful creature I ever saw in my life" (136–37), arousing jealousy and a powerful sense of inadequacy within the narrator.

Working at her desk one day the narrator accidentally breaks an antique Cupid cup and, like a naughty child, hides the pieces, trying to pretend the accident never happened. Mrs. Danvers, however, discovers the broken pieces, confronts Maxim with them, and blames one of the servants while suspecting the narrator. Maxim handles this problem with the same cool efficiency as he handled the extrication of his wife from the overbearing Mrs. Van Hopper, leading the narrator to remark to him, "You are my father and my brother and my son,"

Rebecca 59

a comment remarkably similar to du Maurier's observation about her father in Growing Pains. Maxim treats her very much as if she were his daughter. He suggests that she dress up like a shepherdess for the fancy ball at Manderley or put a ribbon in her hair and be Alice in Wonderland. Several times, in fact, he alludes to her as an innocent, curious Alice. The narrator, on the other hand, asserts: "I wanted to be his wife, his mother. I wanted to be old' (196). The obstacles to her maturity, to her move from daughter to lover and mother, are Rebecca and Mrs. Danvers, whose dynamic and disapproving presences dominate her more than Mrs. Van Hopper ever could. At one point the narrator admits that "I had so identified myself with Rebecca that my own dull self did not exist" (200).

The image of clothing is vital in this story. One day the narrator throws on a mackintosh to go out walking and comes to realize that the jacket belongs to Rebecca. Later, Mrs. Danvers, in showing her Rebecca's room, brings out all of Rebecca's clothes to torment the young girl. She begins by showing her the bed—"It's a beautiful bed, isn't it?" (168), she asks, as if to say that here a real woman enjoyed the sexual act with Maxim, something a mere childish upstart could never hope for. She proceeds to show her Rebecca's furs, nightdresses, even her underwear. "These are her underclothes," Mrs. Danvers says, "in this drawer. The pink set here she had never worn. She was wearing slacks of course and a shirt when she died. They were torn from her body in the water though. There was nothing on the body when it was found, all those weeks afterwards" (169). Mrs. Danvers later suggests that the narrator design her costume for the great ball after that worn by the woman in white in a painting hanging in the house. Not realizing that the painting is that of Rebecca, the narrator unwittingly transforms herself into a caricature of Rebecca. When she makes her grand entrance downstairs, she is greeted by a stunned silence, and Maxim commands that she go and change her clothes. Mrs. Danvers, the malignant designer of this scene, displays "The face of an exultant devil" (214) at the narrator's faux pas.

After the party Maxim does not come to bed with the narrator, and she assumes that her marriage of only three months is a failure. "Rebecca was still mistress of Manderley," she thinks. "Rebecca was still Mrs. de Winter. . . . I could fight the living but I could not fight the dead. . . . Rebecca would never grow old. Rebecca would always be the same. And she and I could not fight. She was too strong for me" (233, 234). Mrs. Danvers reminds the narrator of just how powerful a figure Rebecca was. Having cared for her since she was a child, Mrs. Danvers explains that Rebecca "had the courage and the spirit of a boy," that when she went horseback riding she dug her spurs into the horse's sides drawing blood—"That's how she went at life" (244). "She cared for nothing and no one," she continues, "And then she was beaten in the end. But it wasn't a man, it wasn't a woman. The sea got her. The sea was too strong for her. The sea got her in the end" (245).

Mrs. Danvers, of course, has her facts wrong. Maxim shot Rebecca through the heart and killed her. Mrs. Danvers's relationship to Rebecca, however, is such that she could never allow herself to believe any human being could destroy her. Rebecca was a projection of her own ambitions and sexual drives. She tells the narrator about the wild parties Rebecca threw in her boathouse, the men she met in London and brought up on the weekends: "They made love to her, of course, who would not?" (245). After the parties Rebecca would tell Mrs. Danvers all of the intimate details—what they said and what they did. "It was like a game to her" (245). Like the sexually frustrated and jilted Miss Havisham in Dickens's *Great Expectations,* Mrs. Danvers has created a beautiful woman to break men's hearts.

Du Maurier suggests that Mrs. Danvers's own sexuality is convoluted. Jack Favell, Rebecca's flashy first cousin, who had enjoyed Rebecca's sexual favors in the past, suddenly turns up at Manderley when Maxim and the servants are away. The narrator saw him come to Manderley to visit with Mrs. Danvers, and, while out walking, she looks towards the house and sees them close the shutters when they see her on the lawn. "There was something not right about it," she thinks, and "I wondered what they had been doing in the west wing" (162). Mrs. Danvers appears to extend Rebecca's sexual favors upon Jack. Indeed, her obsession with Rebecca's clothes, her ritual brushing of her hair, her confidence in her sexual games, and Maxim's statement that Rebecca was "not even normal" (127) all suggest that Mrs. Danvers may have enjoyed a lesbian relationship with her.

Mrs. Danvers's demonic possessiveness of Rebecca leads her to try to dispose of the narrator. After the detailed display of Rebecca's room, she turns to the narrator and says, "It's you who ought to be dead, not Mrs. de Winter" and pushes her towards the open window. "Why don't you jump? Why don't you jump now and have done with it? Then you won't be unhappy anymore" (246). As if bewitched by a hypnotic spell, she is about to jump when a rocket goes off signaling that a ship has gone down in the bay. This proves to be the turning point in the story, for in rescuing the sunken ship the men discover *Je Reviens* with Rebecca's skeleton still within it.

Maxim, knowing the truth would now come out, confesses all to his new wife: "She was vicious, damnable, rotten through and through. We never loved each other, never had one moment of happiness together. Rebecca was incapable of love, of tenderness, of decency. She was not even normal" (271). The narrator's response at this point is totally selfish—her fantasy fulfilled, now that her father-lover has revealed his hatred for his first wife: "the rest of me sat there on the carpet, unmoved and detached, thinking and caring for one thing only, repeating a phrase over and over again. 'He did not love Rebecca, he did not love Rebecca.' . . . My heart, for all its anxiety and doubt, was light and free. I knew then that I was no longer afraid of Rebecca" (284, 285).

The fact that Maxim shot Rebecca through the heart does not phase the narrator. Like Julius Lévy, who approved of his father's murder of his wife, she supports her husband in his violent crime, for, after all, it was a crime that assured her of his love. There is another parallel to *The Progress of Julius*. In that novel Julius's wife dies of cancer, freeing him to devote all of his love to his daughter Gabriel. Rebecca also has cancer, but Max does not discover this until after he has killed her. In his final confrontation with Rebecca, she leads him to believe that she is pregnant, possibly with Favell's child, that it could not be proven it was not Max's, and that it would grow up in Manderley, bear his name, and inherit all his wealth when he died. "When I killed her," he tells the narrator, "she was smiling still" (280). It is only later that he learns that she had a malformation of the uterus, which meant that she could never have a child, but that was apart from her disease, a deep-rooted growth, a cancer, that would have killed her within three months. Thus, the sexually alluring Rebecca is incapable of bearing and nurturing a child, a fact that later stimulates the narrator to declare "We would have children. Surely we would have children" (376). It is as if Rebecca's malevolent spirit was punished with a malignant tumor, a cruel parody of a fetus, and that her perverted sexuality leads her to sterility and death. As Maxim says, "She was not normal."

It is only after the inquest, at which Maxim is declared innocent of any wrongdoing, that he discovers Rebecca had cancer. He tells the narrator, 'I believe . . . that Rebecca lied to me on purpose. The last supreme bluff. She wanted me to kill her. She foresaw the whole thing. That's why she laughed. That's why she stood there laughing when she died. . . . It was her last practical joke . . . the best of them all. And I'm not sure if she hasn't won, even now" (374). In any event, Maxim literally gets away with murder and, given the new medical information, feels no guilt for his crime, only a sense of being had.

As Max and the narrator drive back home, he stops to call Frank Crawley, who informs him that Mrs. Danvers left the house shortly after receiving a long-distance telephone call, presumably from Favell. As they make the final approach to Manderley they see the sky lighted up from the flames of the burning building. The fairy tale has an ambiguous ending. Perhaps Favell called Mrs. Danvers, his apparent lover, and told her about the medical report, leading her to burn down Manderley before it could be further desecrated. There is no evidence that she remained within the building. In fact, as the narrator begins her story, she says, "Mrs. Danvers, I wonder what she is doing now. She and Favell" (8), which clearly suggests that they are both still alive and went off together after the fire. Rebecca also continues to live in a curious way. During the drive back to Manderley the narrator falls asleep and in her dream she imagines that she is Rebecca, writing letters, having Maxim brush her hair, but when she looks into the mirror the face she sees is not her own but Rebecca's, and she wakes from her dream screaming. Although the wicked witches, for all practical purposes, are both dead, the narrator, recording her memories many years hence, is still obsessed with the profound malignancy of Rebecca and is compelled to tell her story in the hope that the demon can be contained within the prison of her narrative.

Preoccupied with the notion of realism, the reviewers frequently made the point that *Rebecca* "belongs not to the realistic but to the romantic tradition of the novel,"[3] as if one could possibly mistake the book for an exercise in realism. The *Times Literary Supplement* also observes that "The conventions of a story of this kind are not the conventions of the so-called realistic novel, and it would be absurd to reproach Miss du Maurier for her fine, careless rapture. In its kind *Rebecca* is extraordinarily bold and confident, eloquent and accomplished to a degree that merits genuine respect." But, the reviewer goes on, "It is fair, no doubt, to call this type of fiction 'dope.' But it is no good pretending that everybody would read Tolstoy or Proust if there were no dope literature."[4] Writing in the *Christian Science Monitor,* V. S. Pritchett, after praising the book for the excellence of its melodrama, complains that "There is a very morbid side to this apparently harmless fairy tale" and that the characters and the morality show "the crude unreality of the tale." Pritchett goes on to say, with some self-satisfaction, that if his readers think that he has "crabbed a first-rate entertainment they can comfort themselves with the fact that the great Gladstone loved the work of Marie Corelli and that chaps like me killed Keats."[5] The assumed canon of literary saints, the snobbery, and the sexism that lie behind these reviews are fairly common features of the male literati that ruled the journals and newspapers during the past hundred years and that, to this day, have denied du Maurier her proper place in modern European and American culture.

Some of the women reviewers took du Maurier to task for other reasons. Eleanor Godfrey, in the *Canadian Forum,* is unhappy with "the almost impossibly inept young second wife. . . . For surely not even the most patient and sentimental of readers can refrain from dismissing the heroine as a product of her own nullity." Unable to explain precisely what it is about this novel that disturbs her, Godfrey merely says that beneath "the sincerity of its workmanship there is a nagging hint of mediocrity."[6] This same reviewer refers to Manderley as "Manderby" and never discusses the characters of Rebecca and Mrs. Danvers, both of whom reinforce the narrator's sense of nullity.

Most of the reviews were very positive, including those in the *New Yorker,* the *London Mercury,* the *Atlantic, Punch, Scribner's Magazine,* and the *Spectator.* Two of the critics, however, suggested that the book seems to have been written by an old lady. Rather more perceptive than Ms. Godfrey, John Patton, in the *New York Herald Tribune,* finds the heroine totally credible: "The girl is touching in her shyness, her childish panic fear of her own ineffectiveness, her instinctive self-withdrawal, her indifference to clothes, soundly real in the cowardice which is the fruit of her inferiority complex and brings its cruel and needless punishment."[7]

About a year after the publication of *Rebecca* Germany was to invade Poland, unleashing the dogs of war. With realism of that dimension, it is no wonder that millions of readers in Europe and America made du Maurier's romantic novel a best seller. In 1937, when she began writing the book, du Maurier herself was in Alexandria, Egypt, where her husband was commanding officer of the second battalion,

Grenadier Guards. During the few months she spent in Egypt she drafted an outline of the novel and wrote the first few chapters. They returned to England, and Browning and his battalion were stationed in Aldershot. Reunited with her children and happy in her charming Tudor house, Greyfriars, she returned to her novel. She writes:

This much I can still remember; sitting on the window seat of the living room, typewriter propped up on the table before me, but I am uncertain how long it took me to finish the book, possibly three or four months. I had changed some of the names, too. The husband was no longer Henry but Max—perhaps I thought Henry sounded dull. The sister and the cousin, they were different too. The narrator remained nameless, but the housekeeper, Mrs. Danvers, had become more sinister. Why, I have no idea. The original epilogue somehow merged into the first chapter, and the ending was entirely changed.[8]

The Rebecca Notebook is only about twenty-five pages long, containing brief chapter outlines, some scattered dialogue, and an epilogue. Chapter 3, for example, is outlined simply as follows: "Married, and so to Manderley. The house, the rooms, determined to do well. Mrs. Danvers, such opposition. 'It is a little difficult, madam, for us. You see we were all very fond of Mrs. de Winter' " (RN 7). The final version of the book has twenty-seven chapters and no epilogue. The notebook, however, has twenty-six chapters and an epilogue. Chapter 26 in the notebook reads as follows:

Going towards Manderley. We still have to go away—they take the decision, they go over it all. After all that has happened. Perhaps Rebecca will have the last word yet. The road narrows before the avenue. A car with blazing headlights passed. Henry swerved to avoid it, and it came at us, rearing out of the ground, its huge arms outstretched to embrace us, crashing and splintering above our heads. (RN, 22)

The epilogue is a rather melancholy chapter, set several years after the automobile accident. Maxim is crippled and walks with a cane, and the narrator's face is disfigured. They live in a small hotel on the Mediterranean where their pleasures are simple ones: conversation, reading the newspapers, enjoying their meals. Despite their physical and mental scars, the narrator feels a glow of contentment and can look back upon the past with a certain detachment. She learns that Manderley will open this summer as a country club and wonders, as she does in the final version, what Mrs. Danvers is doing now. Now that Henry is totally dependent upon her for every little thing, she feels self-confident and bold at last. Unlike the heroine in the final version who looks forward to having children, in the epilogue she states, "But we are shorn of our little earthly glory, he a cripple and his home lost to him, and I, well, I suppose I am like all childless women, craving for echoes I shall never hear, and lacking a certain quality of tenderness. Like a ranting actress in an indifferent play, I might say that this is the price we have to pay for our freedom" (*RN*, 26).

However she came to revise the novel, it was a stroke of genius. The burning of Manderley, for example, is Mrs. Danvers's last hurrah. Like Julius, who drowns his cat to keep the Prussians from enjoying it and who drowns his daughter to keep other men from enjoying her, Mrs. Danvers, in burning down Manderley, prevents the narrator from usurping Rebecca's role as mistress of the house. Since Manderley is now no more, the narrator can visit it only in dreams, and the final version of the novel opens with an Alice-in-Wonderland atmosphere, with the narrator venturing down the rabbit hole of time to visit her lost wonderland. Manderley destroyed becomes a place of compelling fantasy with a powerful gravity pulling both the narrator and the reader deep into a mysterious past. Alice, it will be recalled, looked longingly through a door too small for her to enter at a beautiful rose garden. Echoing this passage, du Maurier's heroine opens her story with these words: "Last night I dreamt I went to Manderley again. I stood by the iron gate leading to the drive, and for a while I could not enter, for the way was barred to me" (1).

The epilogue also destroys the sense of hope that fantasy demands. The novel allows the possibility that Maxim and his wife will enjoy a new life, have children, and transcend the malignant influence of Rebecca and Mrs. Danvers. They may bear some mental scars, but with the burning of Manderley there is a liberation from the demons of the past. The myth of the Phoenix comes to mind: out of the ashes arises new life, new dreams. In the first chapter the narrator, recalling Manderley, says, "The house was a sepulchre, our fear and anxiety lay buried in the ruins. There would be no resurrection" (3). She also says that she will not discuss Manderley with Maxim now: "I would not tell my dream. For Manderley was no longer ours. Manderley was no more" (4). By placing these sentiments in the first chapter, however, instead of in an epilogue, du Maurier creates a rich irony. The narrator does tell her dream to the reader and in so doing makes it clear that Manderley will always belong to her and to Maxim. Their destiny is bound up within its walls and in the very act of telling her story she resurrects Manderley from the ashes and makes it hers once again, even its Alice-in-Wonderland rose garden through which she can now walk freely.

Rebecca has become one of the most widely read novels of all time. Contributing to its enormous popularity was the Hitchcock film based upon the book. Du Maurier was unhappy with the screen version of *Jamaica Inn* that was about to be filmed. Thus, when the motion picture producer David O. Selznick showed interest in *Rebecca* she was hesitant to sell the rights. She was, however, persuaded that Selznick exhibited considerable fidelity in his productions of *David Copperfield* and *Anna Karenina,* and she proceeded to sell him the movie rights for $50,000.[9] The screenplay was written by Joan Harrison and Robert E. Sherwood, and the film starred Laurence Olivier as Maxim de Winter, Joan Fontaine as his wife, Judith Anderson as Mrs. Danvers, George Sanders as Jack Favell, and Florence Bates as Mrs. Van Hopper.

Selznick disapproved of Hitchcock's handling of the film from the beginning. Hitchcock wanted to open the picture with a scene in which Maxim, sailing to the Riviera, causes his passengers to become violently nauseated. Selznick called this idea cheap, protesting that "We bought *Rebecca,* and we intend to make *Rebecca,* not a distorted and vulgarized version of a provenly successful work."[10] Selznick also felt that Hitchcock not only discarded the heart of the novel but that he ignored character for facile humor, overlooking the depth of Mrs. Danvers, Maxim, and the second Mrs. de Winter (whom Hitchcock called "Daphne de Winter" in his scripts). Selznick was also outraged to learn that Hitchcock attempted to add a character not in the novel—a lunatic grandmother in a tower of Manderley, an idea he got from *Jane Eyre.*

One of the few elements of the original novel that Hitchcock left unaltered was the conclusion. The Motion Picture Production Code (an arm of the so-called Hays Office), however, would not allow Maxim to emerge, as he does in the novel, unpunished for the murder of his first wife. The Hays Office insisted that her death be attributed to an accident, and Selznick hired Robert Sherwood to revise the conclusion. Instead of having Maxim shoot Rebecca through the heart,

Sherwood has her trip over some rope, fall, hit her head, and die during the scene in which she tells Maxim that she is pregnant with Favell's child.

Sherwood makes another significant change. In the screenplay he has Maxim driving back to Manderley with his agent instead of with his wife, who has remained at home. Favell, meanwhile, telephones Mrs. Danvers several minutes earlier telling her that Rebecca had died of cancer and that now Maxim and his new wife will live happily ever after at Manderley. Before Maxim arrives home there is a scene in Manderley showing Mrs. Danvers walking through the rooms with a lighted candle. At this point the script reads: "She [Mrs. Danvers] looks down at the sleeping 'I' [Maxim's wife] and then turns round into the camera, a mysterious, cunning look on her face which is lit below by the candle she holds. The camera pulls back as she exits the room."[11] When Maxim arrives on the scene his home is in flames, and his wife, along with the servants, is watching the burning building. She runs to Maxim and informs him that Mrs. Danvers is still inside the house and that "She's gone mad. She told me she'd rather destroy Manderley than see us happy here."[12] They then see Mrs. Danvers looking out of the same window from which she had tried to make the young Mrs. de Winter jump. The script reads: "As Mrs. Danvers appears at this window, there is a triumphant and defiant look on her face. Flames shoot up and around her."[13] The flames finally catch her clothing, and the roof crashes in. The camera then focuses upon Rebecca's nightdress case as the fire devours the initial "R" engraved on it. The script ends with the narrator's voice over, declaring that "the devil does not ride us anymore   and both of us are free."[14]

Sherwood's conclusion makes du Maurier's novel morally tidier: the hero commits no crime, and the villain is destroyed by her own hatred and mad possessiveness. The fact, however, is that Maxim does get away with murder, that his wife knows he has killed Rebecca and supports him, and that Mrs. Danvers appears to have escaped from the house unharmed. Both the *Rebecca Notebook* and the novel have the narrator wondering what Mrs. Danvers is doing now. Nevertheless, the ending of the film is richly dramatic, perhaps even more so than the novel. The intervention of the Hays Office is another matter. By disallowing Maxim's murder of Rebecca, the film denies him the satisfaction of his rage as well as his subsequent obsession with his actions.

Richard Kiely, in his book *The Romantic Novel in England,* makes an observation that may help to explain how du Maurier's conclusion to *Rebecca* is historically more in keeping with the tradition of the romantic novel than is the film. Kiely writes: "One might say that a resistance to conclusiveness is one of the distinguishing characteristics of romantic fiction. The memorable scenes and original insights come not in climaxes, which often tend to be melodramatic and unconvincing, but in the prolonged preparation for and ingenious prevention of climax."[15] Even more telling is his following observation: "In its broadest meaning, resistance to conclusiveness is an extension (or an attempted extension) of the ego beyond the limits imposed upon it by time and place. This temporal and spatial restlessness motivates the dominant gestures of romantic fiction—the breaking out and running free and the continuous dreaming and remembering of other times and places."[16] The ambiguity of du Maurier's conclusion reinforces the narrator's dream revisitation of Manderley. The film's conclusion, however, suggests that the past is past, that evil has been vanquished, and that Maxim and his wife can now proceed to live happily ever after. Not so. The nightmarish inhabitants of Manderley continue to haunt the dreams and life of du Maurier's narrator.

The casting of the film presented innumerable problems and led to the rejection of some famous actors who tried out for the major roles. Selznick turned down David Niven as Maxim because he was "entirely too shallow."[17] Before he settled upon the brilliant Judith Anderson for Mrs. Danvers, Selznick had considered Alla Nazimova and Flora Robson for the role. The most difficult part to cast was that of the second Mrs. de Winter. Among those who were tested were Vivien Leigh (Olivier's wife at the time), Loretta Young, Anne Baxter, Margaret Sullivan, Olivia de Havilland, and Joan Fontaine.

Fontaine later explained how Hitchcock helped to shape her brilliant performance:

He wanted total control over me, and he seemed to relish the cast not liking one another, actor for actor, by the end of the film. Now of course this helped my performance, since I was supposed to be terrified of everyone, and it gave a lot of tension to my scenes. I kept him in command, and it was part of the upheaval he wanted. He kept me off balance, much to his own delight. He would constantly tell me that no one thought I was good except himself, and that nobody really liked me and nobody would say anything good about me except himself.[18]

Perhaps because of all the tension between Selznick and Hitchcock and between the various actors, the film turned out to be one of Hitchcock's masterpieces. *Rebecca* won Best Picture in the Academy Awards in 1940, winning over such remarkable films as *The Grapes of Wrath, The Great Dictator, The Long Voyage Home, The Philadelphia Story,* and *Our Town.* Furthermore, the film made du Maurier one of the most famous and sought-after writers of her day and guaranteed her a long and happy career with Hollywood producers and directors.

Most of the reviews of the film are repetitious in their praise for Laurence Olivier, Judith Anderson, and especially for Joan Fontaine. With few exceptions they declare Hitchcock's first American film a successful work of art and entertainment. The exceptions, however, are interesting. Otis Ferguson writes in the *New Republic* that "Rebecca is not really a bad picture, but it is a change in [Hitchcock's] stride and not a healthy one. A wispy and overwrought femininity in it somehow. A boudoir. The first half of the picture just proves that a bright girl who is at home with such words as 'lahst' and 'conservtreh' could continue to be the lady of a house in which she tripped on every stair and bumped into every butler and slipped on every stretch of floor and dropped her gloves or coffee cup or otherwise made a frightful mess every time a superior domestic appeared." "Joan Fontaine," he concludes, "quite lovely as the bride, lived a miniature hell every minute there, and so did I."[19] This sounds more like a review of Carol Burnett's parody of *Rebecca* on her television show rather than one of Hitchcock's film. Indeed, Burnett caricatured the young bride with precisely the overdone clumsiness that Ferguson claims marred the film.

The most interesting analysis of the picture appeared in 1970 in an essay by Raymond Durgnat entitled "Missing Women." Durgnat writes: "The level of characterisation is indicated by the name of the Olivier character—Maxim de Winter, if you please—Maxim indicating his aristocratic grandeur (and fatherly, not to say Oedipal importance), de Winter something of his lost youth, his ravaged bleakness."[20] Durgnat is one of the rare critics to detect the fundamental psychology of both the book and the film: "The heroine fulfills the archetypal female dream of marrying the father-figure who rescues her from the tyranny of the domineering older woman (i.e., mother). But in so doing she has to confront the woman from the past, the woman who possessed her father first, who can reach out and possess him once again."[21] Indeed, the theme of implicit incest that Durgnat observes in the film lies at the heart of du Maurier's earlier books, as we have already seen, and continues into her later work in different forms.

Durgnat's reading of the film confirms and is applicable to the interpretations of nearly all of du Maurier's works presented in this study: "Like many of Selznick's films, *Rebecca* is a rich and ripe example of woman's film, attuned to congenial compromise between the daydreams and dramas of the distaff side. Critics tend to be very dismissive of the woman's film, preferring the equally silly male sentimentalities of the Western, with its wish-fulfillment virility and violence and camaraderie."[22]

The appeal of du Maurier's novel and Hitchcock's film has proved long lasting. *Rebecca* is readily available today in paperback editions, audio and television tape cassettes, and the film is frequently shown on television and in motion picture theaters holding Hitchcock festivals. In the early 1970s *Rebecca* was made into a television film by the BBC and shown in the United States on PBS's "Mystery" series. The television adaptation was by Hugh Witmore, who remained true to the novel, and the film starred Jeremy Brett as Maxim de Winter, Joanna David as his wife, and Anna Massey as Mrs. Danvers. Beautifully filmed on location in England, the series, despite its fidelity to the novel, lacks the intensity and rich melodrama of Hitchcock's masterpiece. In any event, the production allows Maxim to get his revenge at last by shooting Rebecca through the heart, thereby winning the well-deserved applause of millions of viewers, many of whom must have recognized how frustrated he was back in 1940, when he had to settle for Rebecca's misstep.

Despite the literary snobs who will continue to patronize du Maurier's novels and despite the recent group of feminists who see her romances reinforcing traditional female values, millions of readers, especially women readers, continue to enjoy her books and the films based upon her writings. There is emerging now a new body of women critics, such as Kay Mussell, who are writing serious and intelligent studies of romances and who recognize the hypnotic power these works hold over other women. *Rebecca* is the classic gothic romance of the twentieth century and as such will be around long after the high priests and priestesses of the current literary establishment have perished.

Chapter Four
Love, Adventure, and Rebellion

The subject of romantic love is common to practically all of du Maurier's fiction, but the novels she was to write between the years 1941 and 1954 were especially preoccupied with bold, cunning, and assertive women rebelling against their domestic and social confinements, enjoying exotic adventures or establishing a fierce independence. *Frenchman's Creek, The King's General, The Parasites, My Cousin Rachel,* and *Mary Anne* are all illustrative of these themes. In *My Cousin Rachel* and *Mary Anne* du Maurier creates two heroines who master the art of manipulating men, the former being the classic example of a demonic femme fatale and the latter, the actual ancestor of du Maurier, succeeding by her wit, intelligence, and calculating immorality.

These books mark an interesting departure from *Rebecca*. A lesser writer might have been inclined to have exploited the enormous success of that novel, but du Maurier forges ahead with new characters and new themes, though continuing to explore the world of female fantasy that lies at the heart of her popularity. Instead of a brooding, introspective hero like Maxim de Winter, she now develops bold, reckless heroes, such as the pirate in *Frenchman's Creek* and the historical figure of Richard Grenville in *The King's General*. And instead of the gauche, timid second Mrs. de Winter, she now creates independent and fearless characters like Honor Harris in *The King's General* and Mary Anne Clarke in *Mary Anne*.

John Cawelti observes that "The crucial defining characteristic of romance is not that it stars a female but that its organizing action is the development of a love relationship, usually between a man and a woman. . . . Romances often contain elements of adventure, but the dangers function as a means of challenging and cementing the love relationship."[1] *Treasure Island* and *Frenchman's Creek* are both filled with pirate adventures, but the former focuses upon action and danger and does not contain a love interest, while the latter is chiefly concerned with a love story and makes the pirate adventures subsidiary to the romance.

Cawelti offers another generalization that is applicable to some of the novels discussed in this chapter: "The moral fantasy of romance is that of love triumphant and permanent, overcoming all obstacles and difficulties. Though the usual outcome is a permanently happy marriage, more sophisticated types of love story sometimes end in the death of one or both of the lovers, but always in such a way as to suggest that the love relation has been of lasting and permanent impact. . . . There seems little doubt that most modern romance formulas are essentially affirmations of the ideals of monogamous marriage and feminine domesticity."[2] Du Maurier certainly believes in the all-importance of the family unit, but several of her novels, as will be seen, reshape the romance formula in interesting ways. Some of her heroines offer the reader a temporary escape from a boring marriage, involving the reader in an enjoyable fantasy of infidelity. Other of her heroines allow the reader to engage in a fantasy of sinister and deadly control over their lovers.

Frenchman's Creek

One of the most interesting commentaries on *Frenchman's Creek* comes in the form of James Agee's review of the film, based on du Maurier's story. Agee calls the book "a little bathroom classic," saying that "I have always thought—not very originally, I imagine,—that the essence of Madame Bovary and her millions of great-granddaughters is masturbation, literal as often as figurative. This film, like the 'novel' it improves on, is masturbation-fantasy triple-distilled, infallible as any real-life dream and as viciously fascinating as reading such a dream over the terrible dreamer's shoulder."[3] "The shoulder of the actual dreamer here, and of the audience," he goes on, "is unmistakably that of a suburban fat-mama. But on the screen there is magically no such thing: she is an English noblewoman of the Restoration, and lovely to look at, at that." Her country refuge, he observes, is not some little place in Connecticut, but "a whackingly beautiful mansion on the Cornish coast."[4] Her lover, a local pirate, is more of a composite:

With his accent, his gently insolent bearing, and his knowledgeable eyes, he is the sort of European who panics sensitive young matrons by observing that your "American men, sharming and antoozieyestic as they are, know nod-dinx oof lahv"—or, as usefully, by sad-eyed muting of reference to his experience in concentration camps he never saw; at the same time he is easily recognizable as the sort of tousleheaded, briar-sucking commercial artist who fancies himself as a second Gauguin on Sundays, who has gone hermit at $20,000 a year and who threatens every smug harbor on both sides of Long Island Sound with his trim little launch.[5]

Agee stirs himself into an angry tirade against the submerged tale of marital infidelity that lies beneath the dazzling costumes and colors of this work:

None of the unusually resourcefully Technicolor, wax-fruit dialogue, or munificence of costume and social degree conceals the fact that this is really just an archetypally sordid, contemporary middle-bracket flirtation, told without perception, warmth, honor, or irony from the center of a soul like a powder-parlour—but told, in those terms, with the gloves off, and every cowardly emotion and creepy desire and sniveling motive caught red-handed.[6]

This is an entertaining and perceptive reading of both the novel and the film, but what is it about them that disturbs Agee? The heroine is clearly a selfish woman who desperately longs to escape from her boring, asexual, foppish husband and her dull children in order to enjoy adventure on the high and dangerous seas of infidelity. Agee presents himself as one who inadvertently walks into a woman's bathroom and is embarrassed and revolted at what he sees: a middle-class "fat mama" enjoying a masturbatory fantasy. Words like "sordid," "sniveling," and "creepy" reveal his disillusionment with such ordinary, contemporary, middle-class sexuality. Years later John Updike would shape this same subject matter for the fascination of another generation. What seems to disturb Agee, then, is the fact that du Maurier dressed up her sexual fantasy for a costume piece, that she thinly disguised her feelings by draping them with the veil of history, that, in short, she refused to write a realistic novel.

Agee correctly interprets the du Maurier fantasy, but it is the dream and not the interpretation that has the power to enthrall people. Robert Louis Stevenson, combating the trend of realism in the novel years earlier, wrote, "The great creative writer shows us the realization and the apotheosis of the day-dreams of common men. His stories may be nourished with the realities of life, but their true mark is to satisfy the nameless longings of the reader, and to obey the ideal laws of the day-dream."[7] Stevenson's observation captures the essence of du Maurier's success and Agee's complaint.

Frenchman's Creek opens with a comparison of the romantic past with the more tawdry contemporary scene along the Helford River. The third-person narrator imagines a present-day yachtsman dreaming of the past, envisioning the aristocratic and beautiful Dona and her pirate lover in their ship, *La Mouette,* docked in a secret harbor. The frame thus establishes a sort of Alice-in-Wonderland setting for the fantasy story that follows.

Dona, the lovely and capricious Lady St. Columb, flees from the court of Charles II. Jaded by the viciousness and debauchery of her aristocratic surroundings and bored with her stupid husband, she longs to find new life in Cornwall, in her house near the Helford River. From the moment she arrives, she feels a sense of peace and exhilaration. The local gentry assail her with tales of a dangerous French pirate who comes from Brittany to plunder their goods and attack their women. One day, while wandering alone along the river, Dona meets the pirate. Instead of the stereotyped villain, he turns out to be an elegant, courteous, artistic gentleman, and Dona realizes that she has met the one person who will bring her joy, excitement, and love.

Dona does, indeed, represent the frustrated suburban housewife. She is thirty years old, feels that life is passing her by, and holds a "resentment against the futility of her life, those endless suppers, dinners, card-parties, . . . that stupid flirtation with Rockingham, and Harry [her husband] himself, so lazy, so easy-going, fulfilling too well the part of perfect husband with his tolerance, his yawn before midnight, his placid and sleepy adoration. This sense of futility had been growing upon her for many months, nagging at her now and again like a dormant toothache."[8]

The fantasy is further strengthened by the idea of a split personality, one of du Maurier's growing interests. Dona feels that there is another self deep within her, longing to be released to roam, to seek adventure, to find Mr. Perfect: "This other self knew that life need not be bitter, nor worthless, nor bounded by a narrow casement, but could be limitless, infinite—that it meant suffering and love, and danger, and sweetness, and more than this even, much more" (17). This escape to Navron, the house in Cornwall, is not unlike the young du Maurier's own escape from her parents when she went to Ferryside and enjoyed the visits of her cousin. Woman readers, bored with their husbands and their limited lives, could easily identify with Dona because, like them, "in reality it was escape she wanted, escape from her own self, from the life they had led together . . . she had reached a crisis in her particular span of time and existence, and must travel through that crisis alone" (22).

William, the servant at Navron, is another fantasy figure. It turns out that this little man with a "button mouth" works for the French pirate and can keep his mouth closed about the affair that develops between his master and Dona. She first meets the pirate at Frenchman's Creek, a small inlet near Navron where he hides his ship. This vaginal landscape becomes the place where Dona enjoys her secret sexual encounters with the Frenchman: "this creek was a source of enchantment, a new escape, better than Navron itself, a place to drowse and sleep, a lotus-land" (49). Her initial discovery of this cove is described in terms of a girl's first sexual experience: "Then she knew, then she understood—her hands went clammy, her mouth felt dry and parched, and she felt, for the first time in her life, a funny strange spasm of fear" (50). She determines to tell no one of her discovery, "clinging to her guilty knowledge" (51). All of this before she had even set foot aboard ship!

The pirates and their ship also prove to be dreamwork: "It was all different from what she had expected. These men were like children, enchanted with her appearance, smiling and whistling, and she believed pirates to be desperate creatures, with rings in their ears and knives between their teeth" (53). And then there is this amazing line: "The ship was clean" (53). It is as if she were holding her affair in Disneyland. The Frenchman explains that like Dona, he, too, has a double personality. As Jean-Benoit Aubery, he owned estates in Brittany, had money, friends, and social responsibilities. He became bored with his life, however, and found happiness in piracy. Dona, waxing philosophical, says that a man finds happiness in creation, "his happiness comes in things that he achieves. What he makes with his hands, with his brains, with his talents." The Frenchman replies that "women are not idle. Women have babies. That is a greater achievement than the making of a drawing, or the planning of an action" (74). In this dialogue du Maurier is working out her own inner debate on the subject, trying to reconcile her longing for the freedom enjoyed by a man with her conviction that marriage and the family are essential both to the fulfillment of a woman and society.

The image of clothing is very important in this novel and goes to the heart of the heroine's sexual identity. Dona tells the Frenchman how one evening, in order to overcome her boredom, she dressed up in the breeches of her husband's friend and rode out on a horse at midnight to frighten solitary old women. She later disguises herself as a cabin boy to help the Frenchman steal the ship of a local aristocrat. Perhaps du Maurier was familiar with the lives of Mary Read and Anne Bonny, eighteenth-century women who became fierce and courageous pirates. Dona bears a particular resemblance to Anne Bonny, who abandoned her husband in order to elope with a pirate named Rackam and go to sea with him dressed in men's clothes. Dona's changes of costume, however, allow her to enjoy the freedom of a man while retaining her own sexuality. This transvestism is essentially androgynous. It permits Dona temporarily to suppress her sexuality in order to win the aproval of the Frenchman (even as du Maurier sought to win the approval of her father) for her daring feats of independence. Despite this role playing, however, du Maurier acknowledges the limitations of fantasy with this brief lecture from the Frenchman: "You forget that women are more primitive than men. For a time they will wander, yes, and play at love, and play at adventure. And then, like birds do, they must make their nest. Instinct is too strong for them. Birds build the home they crave, and settle down into it, warm and safe, and have their babies. . . . You see, my Dona, there is no escape for a woman, only for a night and a day" (163, 164).

Here is a self-conscious commentary upon fantasy within the fantasy itself. Through the Frenchman du Maurier is saying that one might enjoy the thrill of a sexual affair, enjoy the freedom of a man to explore the sexual horizon, but that in the end, a woman, unlike a man, is not free, that she is controlled by her instincts to build a family, to shape a nation, to be monogamous. The conclusion of the novel confirms this biological interpretation of a woman's destiny.

When Dona returns to Navron after her pirate adventures, she discovers that her husband and Lord Rockingham have arrived to help eradicate piracy from the area. Rockingham suspects that Dona is involved with the Frenchman and, frustrated at her continual rejections of his sexual advances, attempts to kill her. Dona proves to be a formidable opponent: she hits him with a table leg, bites through the palm of his hand, stabs him in the back, and hurls a heavy shield into his face. She finally faints during the ordeal. Her husband comes on the scene, finds Rockingham dead, and believes that the Frenchman killed him. Although the locals capture and imprison the pirate, Dona uses her cunning to help him escape.

Having enjoyed their fantasy escapades, the hero and heroine revert to their other selves. The Frenchman says he may return to becoming Jean-Benoit Aubery, and "The Lady St. Columb will become a gracious matron, and smile upon her servants, and her tenants, and the village folk, and one day she will have grandchildren about her knee, and tell them the story of a pirate who escaped" (269). The cabin boy, Dona points out, "will vigil sometimes in the night, and tear his nails, and beat his pillow, and then he will fall asleep perhaps, and dream again" (269). The sexual fantasy will continue, the sexual frustration will be real, but Dona's loveless marriage will nevertheless prevail, buoyed up occasionally by her memories of an exhilarating infidelity.

Paramount purchased the rights for *Frenchman's Creek* and spent nearly four million dollars, the most that studio had spent in its history upon a single picture, to turn the novel into a lavish costume piece, with location scenes on the California coast made to emulate Cornwall. Released in 1944, produced and directed by Mitchell Leisen, the film starred Joan Fontaine as Dona St. Columb, Arturo de Cordova as the Frenchman, Basil Rathbone as Lord Rockingham, and Nigel Bruce as Lord Godolphin. John Lardner, in the *New Yorker,* is fascinated with Joan Fontaine's memorable killing of Basil Rathbone: "No villain was ever killed deader by a wee slip of a noblewoman. She first flings a chair at his head, then stabs him in the back with a knife. When he persists, ill-advisedly, in crawling up a stairway after her, she drops a suit of armor on him. He lies still after that, all right, but it would take a thorough autopsy to determine which was the blow that got him."[9]

Frenchman's Creek, with its formulaic dreamwork, is a classic modern romance, setting the pattern for thousands of novels to follow. Millions of women have read, enjoyed, and recommended it to their friends. Refusing to admit popular literature, especially popular female literature, into their canon, some high-culture critics label the book as "dope,"[10] thereby separating themselves from the swarm of female addicts whose minds have been overwhelmed by the powerful drug of romance.

What some of these critics actually reveal is their profound fear of women's sexuality. Their anxiety, in turns, leads them to denigrate the heroine's assertion of her sexuality. One critic, for example, writes disparagingly of Dona's pursuit of the pirate: "Stimulated by this philosophic man of action, Lady St. Columb begins to act like a heifer with a burr under her tail."[11] Philip Hartung, writing in the *Commonweal,* complains that even though the standards of morality in 1668 were looser than they are now, "it is still rather embarrassing to watch our heroine, with whom we are supposed to be sympathetic, be so obvious in her pursuit of the handsome pirate. It must be said to the lady's credit, however, that in the finale she remembers her children, if not her husband, and refuses to flee with her more dashing playmate."[12] Du Maurier's formulaic ending, with its emphasis upon fidelity to family and status quo, comforts even her critics.

Frenchman's Creek has "the right stuff" and the proper form, that of an erotic daydream, to make it a paradigm of the successful romance. What it lacks, however, are the dynamic obsessions of *The Progress of Julius* or *Rebecca.* Those two novels, with their oedipal tensions, convey the profound reverberations of an archetypal struggle for identity. *Frenchman's Creek,* on the other hand, seems detached, self-conscious, manipulative. The dreamer seems too awake during her daydream, and we thereby become aware of her when we should be, in Agee's words, cruising "along the coves and peninsulas of adultery." The characters, like their emotions, are shallow, and, as Agee notes, Dona "never once suggests a woman in love or even in confusion; but she does constantly suggest a Vassar girl on a picket line."[13]

Hungry Hill

For her next novel, du Maurier reverted to the format of the dynastic saga used in *The Loving Spirit. Hungry Hill* tells the story of five generations of Irish landowners living under the curse of a man who considered himself a scion of the ancient Celtic kings. The Donovans of Doonhaven, descended into poverty and crime, have always believed that the Brodricks had stolen Hungry Hill from them. When John Brodrick in 1820 announces that the mountain is to be mined for copper, Morty Donovan utters a curse which, like that in a Greek tragedy, extends through the lives of Copper John's sons and grandsons. Du Maurier carries the story through the year 1920, when the Irish rebels burn Clonmere, the Brodrick home, because John Henry, the last of the family, had been seen drinking with the Black and Tans.

The book contains all of the ingredients of a successful television

miniseries: the struggle of powerful capitalists attempting to reform
the lives of ignorant, lawless men of the land; the sordid sexual affair
of Brodrick's alcoholic grandson with one of the wretched, conniving
Donovans—he is eventually found dead with the Bible in one hand
and a bottle in the other; dramatic floods that drown one of the Brodrick girls; thievery and violence; politics and revolutions; and a romantic theme that asserts the inexhaustible resiliency and power of
nature in the face of man's attempts to usurp her dominance. Despite
all of these surefire ingredients, however, the novel is both shallow
and boring. With the possible exception of du Maurier's portrait of
Copper John and his reckless and rebellious grandson, Johnnie, few
of the characters come to life.

This shallow novel was made into an even shallower film, with the
screenplay by Terence Young and du Maurier herself. Directed by
Brian Desmond Hurst, the picture stars Margaret Lockwood, Jean
Simmons, Siobhan McKenna, Dan O'Herlihy, Anthony Quinn, and
Eileen Crowe. The film is best summarized by John McCarten in the
New Yorker: "*Hungry Hill* is an interminable British saga about gener-
ation after generation of a family whose affairs might be of interest
only to someone mentioned in one of their wills."[14]

The King's General

After her heavy-handed and simplistic account of life in Ireland, a
place she clearly does not know well, du Maurier returned in her next
novel, *The King's General*, to the familiar world she understands best:
Cornwall. Once again, the ghosts of Menabilly and its former inhabitants are allowed to roam the landscape of du Maurier's mind. What
gives this story the vitality lacking in *Frenchman's Creek* is du Maurier's deep personal involvement in it. Her obsession with Menabilly,
in fact, stirred her to research the novel. After living in Menabilly
awhile, she was informed that there was a concealed chamber in the
house whose location was unknown. Apparently a former landlord
came upon the forgotten secret room back in 1824 and found a skeleton sitting at a wooden table in nothing but a pair of Cavalier shoes.
He had the skeleton properly buried and the room walled up. Besides
seeking the whereabouts of this hidden chamber, du Maurier set herself the task of constructing an elaborate romantic story that would
plausibly explain the appearance of the skeleton in Menabilly, her
place of secrets.

The plot of this novel is very convoluted and complex and can only be briefly outlined here. The story is set in the time of the Cromwellian wars and centers upon two Cornwall families, the Grenviles and the Harrises. Honor Harris, the narrator, describes the Grenviles as possessing "some quality in the race, some white, undaunted spirit bred in their bones and surging through their blood that put them, as Cornishmen and leaders, way ahead of the rest of us."[15] The Harrises, who live in Menabilly, represent the landed gentry in a much more sober and hard-working fashion.

The novel opens with Honor, an old, crippled spinster, looking out one of the windows of Menabilly and remembering the past, indulging her "autumn melancholy" (7). She vividly recalls her first encounter with Richard Grenvile, already a colonel in the King's Army, on her eighteenth birthday and how, sitting next to him, she became ill from too much wine and roast swan, thus causing him to miss the after-dinner festivities while he sobered her up. Arrogant, swaggering, caring for no one's opinion but his own, handsome, romantic, brave, a military leader, and an older man (he is twenty-eight), Richard is a composite of du Maurier's heroes: her Prince Charming from literature, her bold and dashing cousin Geoffrey, her father, and Boy Browning. Du Maurier dedicated this novel to her husband, citing him as "also a general, but, I trust, a more discreet one." Richard can be lyrical and earthy. When the young Honor tells him that she hated him at first but likes him better now, he replies, "It's hard that I had to make you vomit before I won your approval" (30).

A few days later they secretly meet in an apple tree in the Menabilly garden where, Honor says, "he tutored me in love, and I responded" (36). These arboreal recreations continue, and they soon become engaged. During a hunt a few days later Honor's horse falls into a chasm because Richard's villainous sister, Gartred, deliberately fails to warn her of the danger, and Honor is left a cripple for life. Richard asks her to marry him, but she refuses and vows never to see him again. Richard marries another woman, has a son, and some years later divorces his wife. Meanwhile, his reputation as a skillful but headstrong commander grows, and he is nicknamed "Skellum," German for vicious beast. He does not see Honor again until he visits Menabilly after the Cromwell rebellion has broken out and he is the King's general in the west. He still wants Honor to marry him, but she refuses, preferring to follow him in her litter from camp to camp, until, after his series of defeats, he is exiled to Holland and they are permanently separated.

The secret room in Menabilly plays a prominent role in the story. (One critic notes that more action transpires in this room "than generally takes place in the Yankee Stadium during the entire year.")[16] Richard and his teenaged son, who betrayed his father to the enemy and who is despised by his father as a weakling, are both concealed within this room awaiting a ship to transport them safely to Holland. Honor later receives the message that only one passenger boarded the ship and a note saying "Tell Honor that the least of the Grenviles chose his own method of escape" (294). In a postscript to the novel we are told that when alterations were made to Menabilly in 1824 the workmen found "the skeleton of a young man, seated on a stool, a trencher at his feet, and the skeleton was dressed in the clothes of a Cavalier, as worn during the period of the Civil War" (298). Apparently overcome with remorse for having betrayed his father, the boy shut himself in the hidden room, pulled its stone door shut, and died there.

Honor Harris is a new du Maurier heroine. She is the woman in the wings, watching adoringly her Prince Charming perform on center stage. Although she and Richard enjoy several moments alone together, there is no indication that they have ever gone beyond holding hands. She is, in her own words, "an incurable romantic" (51), enjoying the fantasy of love developed during the long periods of Richard's absence. The fact that Honor was crippled through no fault of her own and that it is she who refuses to marry Richard further strengthens the fantasy. She can never be rejected, and, even though her body is grotesque, Richard will always love her. She is peculiarly asexual, preferring to nurture Richard's weakling son instead of Richard's macho sexuality. She enjoys the best of two roles, playing the subservient adoring daughter to Richard—the rebellious and courageous manager of men and history—and playing the comforting mother to his shadowy son. The narrator of *Rebecca,* it will be recalled, played both roles with her husband, as did du Maurier with her father. As noted earlier, after her father was accused by his wife of infidelity, du Maurier wrote, "I felt then as if he were my brother, or indeed, my son. The father-daughter relationship had entered a deeper phase."[17]

The character of Richard's sister, Gartred, anticipates du Maurier's greatest femme fatale, Rachel, in *My Cousin Rachel*. "Gartred is a law unto herself" (31), says Honor. She describes her "serpent's eyes beneath the red-gold hair, that hard voluptuous mouth" and claims that "Her power to charm was overwhelming" (9). This description conjures up the idea of a lamia, a creature from folklore supposed to be half woman and half serpent, who lured people in order to suck their blood. In the world of du Maurier's romances, such women represent a threat to monogamy, although the monogamous woman prevails. In *Rebecca*, for example, the second Mrs. de Winter finally wins the love of Maxim, and the ghost of the licentious Rebecca is more or less laid to rest. Even though Honor has been rendered an old maid and cripple by Gartred, she declares that "I was happier with my one lover than Gartred ever had been with her twenty" (157).

Although Gartred is Richard's sister, she nevertheless plays the role of the Other Woman whom Honor must defeat. Richard's wife, whom he hates and divorces early in the novel, is never a threat to Honor. The reader can thus enjoy the fantasy that her lover (husband?) will always love her alone despite his casual affairs with other women. Instead of making Gartred a competitor for Richard's love, du Maurier has her exert her malign influence upon Honor's brothers. The effect of the competition is, however, not unlike that found in *Rebecca*. Gartred is a beautiful, aggressive, sexual creature; Honor is plain, passive, and chaste. Pitted against each other on the battlefield of romance—they even play a game of chess together, which Honor wins—the victor embodies the conventional virtues of the ordinary, nonthreatening woman in love with the image of one man. It almost goes without saying that the ordinary married woman reader would find this a satisfying fantasy. Richard's marriage is a failure, he keeps running back to Honor, and the exotic sexuality of Gartred proves to be only skin deep. The conservative theme of this novel not only has a powerful fantasy appeal but it neatly conforms to the morality of the Hays Office, a fact that du Maurier must certainly have kept in mind, although this particular novel was not made into a motion picture.

The Parasites

With the publication of du Maurier's ninth novel, *The Parasites,* in 1949, it was becoming increasingly clear that the academic critics both in England and America would continue to ignore her work. In his review of *The Parasites* in the *New York Times Book Review*, Ivor Brown commented on this slight. His observation is as relevant today as it was over thirty years ago: "When the academic professors of Literature in Our Time assess the leaders in fiction they tend, as I said, to leave Miss du Maurier out. She is so wickedly readable that their intellectual Puritanism is outraged; they would think it a sin to be so entertained. But the public holds an opposite view—and the public in my opinion is mainly right. The business of narrators is to have narrative quality—and here it is—in abundant measure."[18]

The novel has strong autobiographical roots. As Ivor Brown puts it, "Miss du Maurier was brought up on that queer border-country where Mayfair collides with Bohemia. And this collision—of the artistic and the odd with the Philistine and the formal—is the subject of 'The Parasites.' "[19] In this novel du Maurier returns to a modern setting and to her memories as the daughter of a famous actor. The "parasites" for whom the book is named are the three children of the famous Delaneys: Maria, Niall, and Celia. Maria, who has become a well-known stage actress, was the result of Pappy's affair with a Viennese actress; Niall, a composer of dance tunes, was the result of an affair Mama had with a pianist before she met Delaney; and Celia, their half-sister, unmarried, selfless, nursing her father in his decay, is the only legitimate offspring of the Delaneys.

The story begins in the spring of 1949 and is set within a time frame of just a few hours during an afternoon at Farthings, the estate of Maria's husband, Charles. The opening paragraph masterfully creates a sense of unbearable tension that begins to build beneath a surface of decadence and boredom, and it captures the initial clash between the bohemian Delaneys and Maria's aristocratic husband:

It was Charles who called us parasites. The way he said it was surprising, and sudden; he was one of those quiet reserved sort of men, not given to talking much or stating his opinion, unless upon the most ordinary facts of day by day, so that his outburst—coming, as it did, towards the end of the long, wet afternoon, when we had none of us done anything but read the papers and yawn and stretch before the fire—had the force of an explosion.[20]

After his outburst Charles leaves the room, but his remark causes Maria, Niall, and Celia to review their lives, to analyze their relationship, and to fuse the past to the present.

Each chapter moves from the present to the past or from the more distant past to the less distant past, defining the characters through their early relationship to each other and to their parents. In order to suggest the closeness of the three Delaneys, du Maurier employs a point of view rarely used by a novelist—the first person plural. The "we" represents the combined consciousness of the three characters and embodies first, their shared memories of a joyful past and, later, their shared suffering as they mature and are forced to adopt individual lives away from each other.

Niall is a parasite because he lives off his emotional, perhaps sexual, relationship with his stepsister Maria. He also has a parasitic relationship with Freada, an older woman who nurtures his talent for composing popular music. Maria is a parasite because she lives through the fantasy lives of the various characters she embodies as an actress; furthermore, she maintains a symbiotic relationship with Niall. Celia is a parasite in that she draws her strength from the suffering of others. She thus "sacrifices" a normal life in order to nurse her ailing father for many years. He was her protection from the real world and so, too, were her drawings and short stories.

Du Maurier's memories of her and her sisters following in the wake of their talented father as he enjoyed grand opening nights at the theater or charmed his admirers or argued with hotel managers served as the basis for the early background of the fabulous Delaney family. The excitement and adulation that Maria, Niall, and Celia shared during their childhood, however, is cut short with their mother's death. We are told what each of the children was doing just prior to their mother's fatal fall from a cliff. Niall was walking at her side, having earlier come to feel comfortable in her presence for the first time in his life. Celia was in the house drawing pictures when she heard the screaming outside: "the terrible sound of it rang in her ears like a summons from another world" (76). Maria, the character with whom du Maurier most closely identifies herself, had just emerged from a cave with her boyfriend, Michel. Du Maurier describes the cave with explicit sexual connotations: "The mouth of the cave looked mysterious suddenly, inviting. . . . Michel put his hand out to her, smiling, and she took it and held it fast, and followed him into the cave" (81). Her presumed sexual encounter with Michel in the cave, then, is closely associated with the death of her mother.

This novel displays a fantasy of complex psychological strategy. Maria's sexual awakening leads to her mother's death, thereby eliminating both the competition for her father's love and, as her sexual initiation was with a young man, the guilt for displacing her mother. Maria subsequently develops a sexual attraction for Niall, a relationship that suggests incest (although they have different biological parents) since Niall embodies the same devil-may-care, charming qualities of Papa. The Maria-Niall relationship also recalls du Maurier's several references in *Gerald* and *Growing Pains* to the desirability of her father being her brother.

The third component of the "we" in the novel is Celia, that side of the dream-narrator who functions as nurse to Papa and baby-sitter to Maria's children. She is the fat, ugly, sexless female doomed to be responsible so that her beautiful alter ego can be free. Maria's husband, Charles, is the censorious father figure. As du Maurier points out in *Gerald,* her father, despite his own free style of living, was very conservative when it came to the morals and manners of his daughter. And so, at the end of the novel, Charles proclaims his lofty principles, feels he is profoundly wronged by Maria, and announces his plan to divorce her. Charles, it turns out, has fallen in love with another woman.

There is one more twist in this byzantine sexual fantasy. When we last see Maria she is preparing for her performance at the theater. She takes comfort and strength from recalling her father's advice, "Nothing is worth while if you don't fight back" (335). A Frenchman named Laforge comes backstage to ask her to read his new play, hoping to get her to take the part of a duchess. Laforge turns out to be the son of Michel, the young man who years ago took her into the cave. She then receives a telegram from Niall (it is a suicide note), but, since she refuses to open any telegram before a performance, she does not read it. She tells Laforge to come back after the play is over so that they can go to supper and discuss the new play together. And that is the last we hear of Maria. In a curious way, then, the oedipal desire comes full circle. Maria can symbolically reenact the death of her mother with her new lover, the son of Michel. Meanwhile her father and Niall are both dead, Charles is divorcing her, and her own sexuality has wrought a devastating loss of innocence.

In light of du Maurier's statement in 'This I Believe" that the most important thing in life is to maintain the family, the families she describes in her novels are by and large not well maintained. Maria loves her step-brother and not her husband; she does not care for her children and turns them over to her sister, Celia. The families in her earlier novels are also failures, and mothers and mother-figures in particular are short-lived: they are strangled, shot, die of cancer, fall from cliffs, or get divorced. The children who are singled out for special nurturing by these mothers are usually spoiled and rebellious and grow up to be unsuitable fathers or mothers themselves. The real strength in the Delaney family comes from the unity of the children and their devotion to the father (either directly, as in the case of Celia's nursing him through his years as an invalid, or indirectly, as in the case of Maria who seeks his image in other men).

Critics have frequently commented on du Maurier's romantic treatment of her material, but what they usually fail to note is her preoccupation with the subject of incest. Not since Percy Shelley, who shocked people in the early nineteenth century with his depiction of incest in such works as *The Cenci* and *Alastor,* and Lord Byron, with his much publicized affair with his half-sister, has a popular English author dared to examine this taboo topic. Although du Maurier's novels do not contain the usual scenes of sexual passion expected in romances—her fiction has a remarkably chaste surface—they do explore the bizarre twists of sexuality between family members.

In *The Parasites* she shows both Niall and Maria to be incapable of love with other men or women because they are in love with each other. In one episode, Maria calls Niall into her room and shows him her breasts so that he can see how her pregnancy has brought out the pale blue veins. When he telephones her they share a coded language, and he makes reference to enjoying a dish called "Bombay Duck." "I can't wait for Bombay Duck," (281) he tells her, attempting to put off an eavesdropper's understanding of the conversation. Later Maria asks what Bombay duck means, and he reminds her: "Sharing a compartment in a sleeper" (285). He buys her a negligee for a present, and later, during a dinner party, he sees Maria enter the room as a tenor sings "Pale hands I love." "She had dressed in a hurry," the narrator reports, "she wore nothing, Niall knew, under her dressing-gown affair, which was velvet and the color of old gold. . . . He wondered if it was an oddity with him, approaching perversion, or the familiarity of years of love and knowledge that made him want her most when a little rumpled as she was now, or drowsy on first waking, or greasy with her hair in pins, her make-up wiped away" (297). This was pretty heady stuff for 1949, and even in the 1980s many publishers shy away from this ultimate taboo.

The chief weakness with this novel comes at the conclusion, when Niall decides to commit suicide by going off to sea in a small boat, knowing full well that he would survive only by accident. Niall is depicted as so impractical that we wonder how he ever got the boat out of port to move towards his romantic suicide. Furthermore, we are at a loss to explain how the "we" who narrate the story can possibly know what Niall is doing out there when he is all alone. The point of view occasionally slips into that of an omniscient narrator.

This is, nevertheless, a remarkable novel of introspection and analysis. It resembles a play framed by Charles's judgment of the Delaneys and by his announcement at the conclusion of his plans to divorce Maria. Within the few hours of tense conversation and reflection, the Delaney offspring come to life and reveal their unique solidarity. Through them du Maurier proclaims the power of fantasy and illusion over reality and practicality. The unorthodox, amoral, and artistic Delaneys, committed to each other and to their genius and insulated from mundane concerns, are elevated to the level of bohemian sainthood, while Charles, with his rigid principles and conventional morality, is doomed to the dull routine of upper-class married mortals.

My Cousin Rachel

Du Maurier draws upon the structure of *Rebecca* and the character of Gartred from *The King's General* for her next novel, *My Cousin Rachel,* an intriguing story of a mysterious and dangerous woman. *Rebecca* is about a dominating man and his wife who dies before the story opens. *My Cousin Rachel* is about a dominating woman and her husband who dies before the story opens. The narrator of *Rebecca* falls in love with the powerful and mysterious Maxim de Winter, while the narrator of *My Cousin Rachel* falls in love with the hypnotically seductive and mysterious Rachel. Set in the Ashley estate on the coast of Cornwall, *My Cousin Rachel* conjures up the same brooding atmosphere as *Rebecca*. There the similarity stops. Du Maurier develops the character of Rachel along the lines of Gartred Grenvile, making her new heroine much more sinister and ambiguous.

The novel, narrated by Philip Ashley, is set sometime in the nineteenth century. Orphaned as a young child, Philip was raised by his wealthy cousin, Ambrose Ashley. Shy and mistrustful of women, Ambrose raised Philip in a house from which he has forbidden all women; even the servants had to be men. This situation allows du Maurier to create a narrator whose knowledge and judgment of

women is seriously flawed, thereby establishing an intriguingly ambiguous portrait of Rachel as a femme fatale. As an adult now, about
to become a member of Parliament and a respected landowner, Philip
knows that he will always be haunted by the question he can never
answer: "Was Rachel guilty or innocent?"[21] This proves to be the central unanswerable question of the novel itself.

Philip's story really begins when his cousin, at age forty-three, is
ordered by his doctor to winter in Italy. Shortly thereafter he writes
Philip a letter stating that he has made the acquaintance of a mutual
cousin, part English and part Italian, whose husband, an Italian no-
bleman named Sangalletti, died in a duel, leaving her with huge
debts and a large and empty villa. Before too long Ambrose writes
that he has married her. Philip becomes jealous of Rachel, afraid that
his life-long friendship with Ambrose and the house and property will
all be lost to him. Another letter then arrives that raises the pitch of
the tension: "For God's sake come to me quickly. She has done for
me at last, Rachel my torment. If you delay, it may be too late"(33).

When Philip arrives in Italy he discovers that Ambrose has already
died and that Rachel has left the country leaving no word as to her
whereabouts. Philip then tracks down a man named Rainaldi, who
looks after Rachel's business affairs, and is told that Ambrose probably died of a brain tumor. Philip, however, convinced that Rachel
killed his cousin, does not believe the Italian and vows revenge.
Philip begins to imagine Rachel as a femme fatale: "Her eyes were
black as sloes, her features aquiline like Rainaldi's, and she moved
about those musty villa rooms sinuous and silent, like a snake" (58).

Twenty-four years old, Philip has to wait for his next birthday before inheriting Ambrose's property and wealth. Rachel then lets it be
known that she is planning to come to England. Seeking his opportunity for revenge, Philip asks her to come to the house. He subsequently begins to fear the prospect of a woman entering the Ashley
estate: "an unknown, hostile presence, stamping her personality upon
my rooms, my house. She came as an intruder to my home. I did not
want her. I did not want her or any woman, with peering eyes and
questing fingers, forcing herself into the atmosphere, intimate and
personal, that was mine alone" (80). His language clearly reflects his
fear of her sexual invasion of his mind and body. After all, she had
already apparently destroyed his alter ego—for Philip, observing a
portrait of Ambrose, comments, "We could be brothers though, almost twin brothers" (78).

Upon first seeing Rachel, Philip is shocked that she is so small—
she barely reaches his shoulder. She is dressed in black, lace at her
throat and wrists, has brown hair parted in the center with a low knot
behind, and has large eyes. Somewhat reminiscent of Mrs. Danvers,
she is thirty-five years old. Rachel is continuously associated with gardens, saying, for example, that Ambrose told her that she would
"shrink and shiver in the English climate, especially the damp Cornish one; he called me a green-house plant, fit only for expert cultiva-
tion, quite useless in the common soil. I was city-bred, he said, and
over-civilised" (88). Towards the end of the novel we discover that
Rachel is an expert in herb lore, a talent she acquired from her
mother. Du Maurier may have drawn upon Nathaniel Hawthorne's
"Rappaccini's Daughter" for her portrayal of Rachel. Rappaccini's
garden contains poisonous herbs that he has fed to his daughter, al-
lowing her to build up a tolerance for the toxins but making her a
lethal woman for a young man to know.

During the next few days Rachel and Philip are drawn closer together. Philip's growing affection for Rachel is constantly tested,
however, when he discovers scraps of letters from Ambrose. One of
them enigmatically reads, "I cannot any longer . . . let her have command over my purse, or I shall be ruined, and the estate will suffer"
(170–71). We, like Philip, are given just enough clues to make us
suspicious that Rachel poisoned Ambrose for his money, but du
Maurier never gives us enough information to know for sure. In fact,
Rachel's impoverishment and rejection of an allowance Philip offers
her seem to testify to her innocence.

Philip discovers another letter from Ambrose in one of his coats
that Rachel returned to the estate. It reads: "the loss of our child,
only a few months on its way, did her irreparable harm" (218). Ambrose says that he suspects that Rainaldi has been in love with Rachel
for years, even when Sangalletti was alive, and concludes: "One
thought possesses me, leaving me no peace. Are they trying to poison
me?" (221). This letter drives Philip to have another frank discussion
with Rachel, and she manages to assuage his anxieties leaving him
more convinced than ever of her innocence. He finally hires a lawyer
to arrange to leave all of his inheritance to her upon his twenty-fifth
birthday.

On the eve of his birthday, Philip grows excited, goes to the
beach, and plunges into the cold water. "My mood of exaltation held
me in thrall," he says. At midnight he gives her the legal document

granting her all his lands and house, and then, through an orgasmic
shower of jewels, he declares his love for her—a scene reminiscent of
Jay Gatsby's excited presentation of his shirt collection to Daisy:

> I emptied the packages upon the bed and cast the wicker basket on the floor.
> I tore away the paper, scattering the boxes, flinging the soft wrappings ev-
> erywhere. Out fell the ruby headpiece and the ring. Out came the sapphires
> and the emeralds. Here were the pearl collar and the bracelets, all tumbling
> in mad confusion on the sheets. "This," I said, "is yours. And this, and
> this. . . ." And in an ecstasy of folly I heaped them all upon her, pressing
> them on her hands, her arms, her person. (265)

There is a bizarre sexuality in this scene. All of Philip's erotic emotions are translated through his material possessions onto the bed-
sheets and upon Rachel's body. His tutelage under the woman-hating
Ambrose has not prepared him for this moment, and his stunted sexuality expresses itself through the legacy of his "twin," Ambrose. In
his naivete he never really makes clear his intentions to marry her,
and later Rachel rightly denies that she ever accepted any proposal of
marriage, saying that she merely wanted to thank him for giving her
the jewels. Philip puts his hands around her throat and comes close
to strangling her but then relents.

During the next few days Philip becomes seriously ill and experiences weeks of delirium. He vaguely recalls being nursed by Rachel
who made him drink a bitter liquid. Before long we find him in exactly the same situation as Ambrose, an apparent victim of Rachel
and her deadly herbs. Philip continues to rationalize the situation and
concludes that there are two Rachels: "Perhaps she was two persons,
torn in two, first one having sway and then the other" (335). Once
again he feels a strange, terrible compassion for her. Snooping in her
room, he discovers a letter to her from the bank thanking her for the
return of the Ashley jewels, which, according to her instructions, will
remain in custody with the bank until such time as her heir, Philip,
may take possession of them. He also finds a letter to her from Rainaldi telling her that if she cannot bring herself to leave the boy behind, then bring him with her, though he warns her that such a plan
is against his better judgment.

These revelations make Philip doubt if Rachel is guilty at all, but
he confesses that he will never know for sure. While looking out the
window, he suddenly remembers a workman warning him not to
walk on the bridgeway across the sunken garden because it is only a

framework that will not bear a person's weight. He knowingly allows Rachel to walk out on the lawn toward the bridge. After she has gone for a half hour he suddenly senses she has had an accident and runs out towards the bridge. By the time he arrives she has already fallen to her death.

We are thus left to decide for ourselves whether Rachel was innocent or guilty. Du Maurier has carefully portrayed her narrator as a man whose naivete and undeveloped sexuality make him a confused and oftentimes unreliable narrator. Like Ambrose before him, he becomes paranoid, convinced that the household is in league against him. Sharing Ambrose's unfamiliarity with and mistrust of women, Philip is particularly hard-pressed to understand Rachel, coming as she does from a foreign culture and having fallen from aristocratic wealth to genteel poverty. He is like a teen-age romantic experiencing his first love affair with an older woman, and he responds with all the intensity and melodrama of youthful egotism. Indeed, Rachel may be the victim of his and Ambrose's paranoia.

Du Maurier's technique is here neither unusual nor gimmicky. This novel is very much like one of Robert Browning's dramatic monologues, in which the narrator presents the "facts" through his limited and oftentimes misguided perceptions, revealing his own character more fully than that of the people he describes. This technique captures the rich ambiguity of life itself, the hazy border between fact and fantasy, truth and illusion.

A typical review of the book concludes, "It's a safe bet that the truth about Rachel will be a prime teatime topic at women's clubs this winter. Did she poison her husband with laburnum seeds, or was she just the charming woman of the world she seemed to be? We shall probably have to wait for Hollywood to get the answer."[22] Hollywood, however, retained the ambiguity of the novel—no small feat since the story could no longer be told from the first-person point of view—and produced an exciting, well-cast and well-acted motion picture.

The film starred Richard Burton (an actor new to Hollywood) as Philip and Olivia de Havilland as Rachel. Bosley Crowther, in the *New York Times,* welcomed this "excellent screen translation of Daphne du Maurier's literate romance."[23] The lean and handsome Burton is the perfect hero for this picture. His adolescent outbursts of ecstasy and torment are in the grand romantic style of the novel. Olivia de Havilland is also a piece of creative casting. Although she fails to capture the exotic Italian character of Rachel, she more than makes up for this in her brilliant ambiguity. Her face displays innocence, wonder, and tenderness, but her actions suggest her sinister entrapment of Philip. When she turns on Philip after he bequeaths all his riches upon her, she becomes demonic and frightening.

Having experimented with the perspective of a paranoid male who attributes to a woman powers that she may not in fact possess, du Maurier, in her next novel, goes all out in her straightforward portrayal of a woman who seduces and exploits men in order to satisfy her hunger for power and win a certain amount of security for herself and her children.

Mary Anne

Mary Anne is set in England during the latter part of the reign of George III, the period when he was becoming progressively insane. By 1818 he was considered permanently mad, and the prince of Wales (later George IV), the first son of George III, was made regent and ruled England. Frederick Augustus, the duke of York, was the second son of George III. He commanded the unsuccessful English forces in Flanders during the French Revolutionary Wars. He was more influential at home, where he was active in reforming abuses in the army. As commander in chief, he led another disastrous expedition to the Netherlands against France. He resigned his command in 1809 after he was acquitted of selling army commissions through his mistress, Mary Anne Clarke.

Du Maurier examined diaries, letters, newspapers, and other accounts of this tumultuous period of English history before she set out to write the story of her great-great-grandmother. Nevertheless, the history quickly fades into the background as du Maurier develops her character study of an ambitious woman who has the wit, audacity, and the ability to play upon masculine weakness for her own advantage. Vaguely reminiscent of Defoe's Moll Flanders and Thackeray's Becky Sharp, Mary Anne is a modern-day Cinderella who rises from the slums of London to become one of the most influential women in England.

Written from the omniscient point of view, the novel opens with Mary Anne, age seventy-six, at the window of her house in Boulogne, looking across the Channel to the England that had forgotten all about her. The duke of York is dead, the scandal long passed, her favorite daughter is dead, and her grandchildren, whom she had nursed as babies, are ashamed of her and never write. "The men and women she had known had passed into oblivion. The dreams were all hers."[24] The rest of the novel is a flashback to Mary Anne's ample life.

Once again du Maurier presents an image of a mother who is weak and ineffectual, driving her daughter to seek men as role models. Du Maurier writes of Mary Anne: "The first thing to remember was not to grow up like her mother, who was weak, who had no resistance, who was lost in this world of London that was alien to her, and whose only consolation was to talk of the past, when she had known better days" (23). "When I grow up," Mary Anne says, "I shall marry a rich man." When asked how she will set about this plan, she replies, "By making a fool out of someone . . . before he makes a fool out of me" (24).

Du Maurier's youthful dream of becoming a boy—"Why wasn't I born a boy? They did all the brave things. Fought all the battles"[25]— underlies the character of Mary Anne. As a young girl Mary Anne finds that men's talk is more interesting than that of women. Instead of talking about babies, housekeeping, and the neighbors, they discuss the state of the army, the rebels in France, and other grand matters.

After her stepfather, Bob Farquhar, runs off with another woman, Mary Anne proceeds to take charge of the family's finances and arranges to take in a tenant to help them pay the rent. The tenant turns out to be a handsome, arrogant young man named Joseph Clarke. Mary Anne falls in love with him, and on her sixteenth birthday they get married. Like Moll Flanders, she discovers only after the marriage that he is not wealthy as she had assumed. With the help of Joseph's brother, Mary Anne sets her husband up in the stone masonry business, but he proves a miserable failure at the trade. Meanwhile, she has given birth to three children and has a baby on the way.

Joseph's brother commits suicide after he loses his life savings in a speculation urged upon him by Joseph. With her financial security now undercut, Mary Anne "saw her life merging into that of her mother, repeating the same pattern. A baby every year. Malaise, irritation. The four little faces round the table mimicking the past . . . dependent upon her, never upon Joseph. Joseph turning into her stepfather Bob Farquhar in nightmare fashion, sleepy-eyed, blotched, always an excuse upon his lips. How break away, escape? How defeat her mother's image?" (75).

Like Dona, in *Frenchman's Creek,* Mary Anne experiences the frus-
trations of a woman whose freedom has been impaired by an unsatisfactory husband and a brood of children for which she is responsible.
But whereas *Frenchman's Creek* provides the woman reader a means of
escape from her own dull reality by engaging her in a sexual fantasy,
Mary Anne offers her a different, but related and perhaps equally satisfying, fantasy—that of indomitable power over men.

Armed with a knowledge of men and despising the role of her
mother, Mary Anne begins her relentless climb up the social ladder
by becoming a high-class prostitute. She works for a man who has
only the cream of society, including the Prince of Wales, as his clients. Meanwhile, an honest, hard-working man named Bill Dowler—
who appears to be modeled after the dull but loyal Dobbins in Thackeray's *Vanity Fair*—becomes Mary Anne's faithful confidant. Mary
Anne brashly informs him that she cannot wait until his father dies
to inherit the money she needs right now: "You'll inherit false teeth
and a wig, and I'll be bald-headed. I have to live now" (100).

As Mary Anne begins to gather her wealth, she has her mother and
children move in with her, and she continues to practice discreetly
her sexual trade with distinguished visitors. Having lost her son from
the measles, she becomes more determined than ever to provide for
the security of her family: "I had a son who died. . . . I made a vow.
I'll play any game in the world that a woman can; if it's sordid, or
dirty, or mean, I don't give a damn . . . and heaven help any man
who lets me down" (116). Her game finally leads her to become the
mistress of the duke of York, and she thinks, "I've arrived . . . I've
reached the top. . . . The question is . . . how long can I hold the
job?" (130).

When the duke does not give her an adequate allowance to pay for
all her servants, grooms, and coachmen, she begins to accept bribes
from military personnel desiring promotions. She raises their names
while she is in bed with the duke and easily obtains his promise to
grant the promotions. By trading on her sexual favors in this fashion
she is able over the next few months to amass a fortune and to wield
enormous social influence. She learns to relish the control she now
holds over the fates of hundreds of men. "This was power and enchantment in one," she thinks, "it was bliss, it was nectar" (163).
She begins to look to the day when the duke succeeds his father as
king (praying that both the sickly Prince of Wales and his wife die,
opening a path for the duke)—"Then . . . what a blaze! What a future!" (163).

Disaster soon strikes, however, and the duke is investigated by the House of Commons on charges that he is guilty of selling promotions. The investigation fascinates the entire country, and Mary Anne becomes a notorious national figure. Although the duke is exonerated by the House, the vote reveals a small majority. In the eyes of the public he is considered suspect, and he resigns his position as commander in chief. In a desperate attempt to win patronage for her son, Mary Anne publishes an attack upon the Chancellor of Ireland and is tried for libel. "Mary Anne has overreached herself at last" (359), we are told. Sentenced to nine months imprisonment, she quotes Mary Stuart, "In the end is my beginning. . . . I think we've arrived" (367).

Although she has been banned from England, when Mary Anne reads in the newspapers that the duke has died, "some stubborn, fundamental English pride drove her to cross the Channel once again" (378) to attend his funeral. She obtains only a glimpse of his sword. One of the people on the street asks her if she came far to see the funeral. She replies, "Only from round the corner, from Bowling Inn Alley" (378), the London slum in which she was born. Like Mary Stuart, she has come full circle.

Du Maurier's presentation of Mary Anne elicited widely differing responses from the reviewers. Geoffrey Bruun, in a front-page essay in the *New York Herald Tribune Book Review,* for example, sees Mary Anne as a "lively lady."[26] Bruun clearly recognizes du Maurier's technique of romanticising history so as to present a heroine larger than life, one capable of fulfilling the fantasy of the female reader to hold power over men and to beat them at their own game. An anonymous reviewer in the *Catholic World,* on the other hand, finds du Maurier's treatment of her heroine nasty and immoral: "Miss du Maurier's interest is in the boudoir rather than in the budget. Mrs. Clarke is portrayed in a nasty, sniggering way and with enormously misplaced sentiment. She is no Becky Sharp, whatever the author's intention, and there is no relief or perspective, as in Thackeray's novel, through which her activities and character are seen for what they really are. A slipshod and thoroughly unpleasant book."[27]

Whatever moral judgments Thackeray's clever narrator may make about Becky Sharp's character, the fact remains that he makes Becky a much more interesting and engaging character than he does the morally proper Amelia. Du Maurier obviously sympathizes with her rebellious heroine and justifies her actions. Like Robert Browning, she prizes characters who take their destinies into their own hands and boldly face the challenges put before them by the institutions, customs, and mores of their time.

Du Maurier may not be a masterful prose stylist, but she is very effective, indeed, when it comes to enveloping her women readers in her own fantasies. Not only does *Mary Anne* capture the exciting fantasy of a woman's indomitable power over men, it also places that fantasy within a realistic context that demonstrates the transient nature of such power. As the opening quotation shows, Mary Anne, at age seventy-six, lives alone, abandoned by her children. Her lovers are dead, her glory has passed, and the "men and women she had known had passed into oblivion. The dreams were all hers" (20). Like Mary Anne, the reader knows the transience of her own fantasies and can sympathize with the aged heroine, knowing they share a common dream of a world brighter than the present one.

Dona St. Columb, Honor Harris, Maria Delaney, Rachel, and Mary Anne all exhibit du Maurier's fascination with romantic love, rebellion, adventure, and power. These characters are at their best when they are in the company of strong men, such as the Frenchman, Richard Grenvile, or the duke of York. Weak male characters, however, abound in the novels, and the heroines easily overcome whatever obstacles they may put in the way of their quest for love or power. Dona, for example, keeps her foolish husband at bay while she is enjoying her affair with the pirate and kills the meddling Rockingham when he attempts to intrude upon her adulterous adventure. Similarly, Ambrose and Philip Ashley are no match for their sophisticated and mysterious cousin Rachel. At the heart of all of the novels discussed in this chapter are a series of strategies for attaining some form of sexual fulfillment, freedom, or dominance over men. An adulterous fantasy in *Frenchman's Creek*, the supremacy of mother earth over several generations of attempted male dominance in *Hungry Hill*, the sublimated sexuality of a deformed woman who nurtures her lover and his son in *The King's General*, the incestuous love between a young woman and her step-brother in *The Parasites*, the femme fatale in *My Cousin Rachel*, and the more open use of sex as a means to power and wealth in *Mary Anne* all underscore du Maurier's obsession with these themes. Finally, du Maurier's relationship with her mother and father provides the emotional energy that helps bring to life the curious creatures who inhabit the romantic and sometimes bizarre world of her imagined Cornwall.

Chapter Five

The Search for Identity

Du Maurier's last five novels, *The Scapegoat* (1957), *The Glass-Blowers* (1963), *The Flight of the Falcon* (1965), *The House on the Strand* (1969), and *Rule Britannia* (1972) reveal her growing interest in psychology and the question of identity. Each of these works takes a different perspective on psychodynamics as du Maurier explores the theme of the double in *The Scapegoat,* the shaping influence of family history upon one's identity in *The Glass-Blowers,* the nature of the demonic self in *The Flight of the Falcon,* the influence of mind-altering drugs upon one's sense of reality in *The House on the Strand,* and the importance of family and national identity in *Rule Britannia.* Although the settings for these works extend to France and Italy, du Maurier's focus is firmly upon the bizarre twists of the psyche. In her last two novels, however, her own profound sense of place leads her back to the romantic and hypnotic history of Cornwall, the land that first inspired her to become a writer. The past has the power to consume the present and to take on a reality of its own. Paraphrasing Mary Stuart, du Maurier writes, "In my beginning is my end, and having passed through many phases and attempts to be other than I am, I have reached my fifty-eighth year with the realisation that basically I have never changed."[1] The heroine of her last novel, an old woman named Mad, embodies the brave spirits of du Maurier's earlier heroines, this time fighting to preserve Cornwall against foreign invaders. In a sense, this book is du Maurier's last testament. In Mad's battle to defend Cornwall against the invading Americans we see du Maurier's strong territorial imperative as she fights off the barbarians who would dare to invade her mythic world, peopled over many decades with the cherished ghosts of her romantic imagination.

The Scapegoat

The narrator of *The Scapegoat* is a middle-aged historian named John, who is spending the summer in France collecting notes for the series of lectures he is to deliver to his London students. Although he speaks fluent French and has a thorough understanding of French history, he laments that he was never intimately involved with the people of France: "I was an alien, I was not one of them."[2] He views himself as a failure even though his friends and colleagues consider him a competent scholar. At the heart of John's dissatisfaction is his sense that there is another personality within himself that has not had the opportunity to develop.

John pauses for a drink in Le Mans where he meets a stranger who is his double. The stranger, whose name is Jean de Gué, proposes that they exchange their clothes and their lives. Either drunk or drugged, John passes out. When he awakens the next morning he finds Jean gone and Jean's chauffeur waiting for him. "He was my shadow or I was his," John thinks, "and we were bound to each other through eternity" (23). And so, John heads out for his new life: "I was wearing another man's clothes, driving another man's car, and no one could call me to account for any action. For the first time I was free" (34).

Ably assisted by Gaston, the chauffeur, John decides to carry the masquerade as far as he can. When he arrives at the chateau, he learns that he must quickly accommodate himself to Jean's peculiar family. Since Jean was notorious for his bizarre behavior, no one questions his double's initial awkwardness. Jean's daughter, Marie-Noel, is a high-strung, eleven-year-old girl who reads the lives of the saints and sees visions. She tells John that if he hadn't come home she would have committed suicide by leaping out the window, "And then I should have burnt in hell. But I would rather burn in hell than live in this world without you" (71). Jean's younger brother, Paul, is married to Renée, who tries to seduce John. Jean's pregnant wife, Françoise, is a neurotic, complaining woman, and John makes up a series of excuses not to sleep with her during his week-long adventure at the chateau. Jean's sister, Blanche, has not spoken to him in fifteen years. Jean's mother, Madame la Comtesse, is bedridden and addicted to morphine.

Jean runs a glassblowing company that is on the verge of bankruptcy. Unlike his double, who does not care if the company closes down, John visits the workers, develops a compassion for them, and begins to work out ways to keep the business operative. He starts to wonder if Jean left his life behind because he did not care or because he cared too much. "What was happening, then," John reasons, "was that I wanted to preserve Jean de Gué from degradation. I could not bear to see him shamed. This man, who was not worth the saving, must be spared. Why? Because he looked like me?" (114). He begins to feel that his actions are drawing him closer to his double, "whose inner substance was part of my nature, part of my secret self" (138). The character of Jean's mistress, Béla, allows the narrator to unburden his thoughts. She becomes his confidante and appears to understand his Jekyll-and-Hyde personality. Béla is one of those characteristic du Maurier women who play many roles: "The Béla of Villars completed a pattern, a pattern containing mother, wife, and child. The warmth of one, the dependence of the second, the laughter of the third, shaped themselves to make a fourth of her, and, finding this, I lost myself in all. Here was a part of the solution, but not the whole" (167).

The novel proceeds in the manner of a detective story with the narrator piecing together numerous clues to come to some understanding of the mystery enveloping this family. He learns that Jean had the former master of the glassblowing business, a man by the name of Duval, murdered because he believed that Duval was attempting to obtain control of the company by marrying Blanche. Suspecting that Jean was behind Duval's death, Blanche had never spoken to him since. Blanche's sorrows turned inward, and she became a masochistic religious fanatic: "the Cross she knelt before in her bedroom was not a Saviour but her own hope crucified" (260). John senses that she is attempting to turn Marie-Noel, whom she thinks she is saving, into a victim of her own misery. This relationship puts us in mind of Dickens's Miss Havisham in *Great Expectations,* who after she is jilted converts her frustrated sexuality into a program of hatred for her protégé, Estella.

The turning point in the novel comes when Françoise falls or jumps to her death from a window. John is suddenly overcome by a sense of responsibility for all of the misery that has befallen this family. John then helps the Comtesse to face her drug addiction and encourages her to take over some of the family responsibilities. He confronts each member of the family with his or her involvement in Françoise's suffering and death, but goes on to show how, with the help of the settlement of her will, each can derive new purpose and hope. He persuades Paul to travel and obtain orders for the factory, relieving him and Renée of their boredom and self-destructive impulses. He convinces Blanche to manage the business. Working together, he argues, they will save not only their own identities but the family tradition. John soon has everyone humming with a purpose. Even Marie-Noel, who had attempted suicide a few days earlier, is now happy because "I haven't been saddled with a baby brother after all but have you [John] to myself for the rest of my days" (333).

Having now brought hope and peace to the family, John receives a phone call informing him that Jean is about to return home. John feels "I was the possessor now, he the intruder. The chateau was my chateau, the people were my people, the family . . . my family" (336). To protect his new identity, John plans to kill his double when he returns: "I was the substance now and he the shadow. The shadow was not wanted and could die" (340). A local priest, however, comes upon John waiting with a pistol at Duval's former house and disarms him, thinking he was about to take his own life. "By living you can create the world afresh" (343), he tells him.

Shortly after the priest leaves, Jean arrives and holds John at gunpoint. "You've succeeded in living a lie for seven whole days," he says and proceeds to mock with bitter cynicism John's noble attempts at reforming the family. He accuses John of being an incurable sentimentalist when he says he loves Jean's family. He then gives John a brutally cynical character sketch of each family member and explains how he has uprooted John's life in London by spending all of his money, resigning his position at the university, giving up his lease on his apartment, and selling all of his furniture. "The self who had lived in London had gone forever" (355), John thinks. All the while the two men are talking in the dark, suggesting a symbolic inner debate.

Jean decides not to kill his double but changes clothes with him, says he would be delighted to exchange identities again at some later date, and returns home to be embraced by Marie-Noel. John goes to Béla, who suspects that his other self has returned. She explains that John's influence upon her and the family will be a lasting one, that Jean is not a devil, but an ordinary man. She tells John, "You've given something to all of us . . . tendresse. Whatever it is, it can't be destroyed. It's taken root. It will go on growing. In the future we shall look for you in Jean, not for Jean in you" (365). John simply says that he has finally learned what to do with failure: turn it into love. Now, he wonders, "What do I do with love?" (367). He kisses Béla goodbye and drives off towards the Foret de la Trappe, to visit a monastery. Although his purpose in heading towards the abbey is left ambiguous, there is the suggestion that, now that he has discovered his inner self and has displaced a sense of failure with a realization of the power of love, he may become a monk.

Reviewers were very free with their praise of *The Scapegoat*. Most of them willingly suspended their disbelief when it came to accepting du Maurier's fantastic premise that one man could successfully exchange his identity with that of a stranger. Anthony Boucher, in the *New York Times Book Review,* says that "The concept of the impostor . . . is one of the most absorbing premises in fiction; and Miss du Maurier's John . . . joins a succession of great maskers, from Anthony Hope's Rudolf Rassendyll to Josephine Tey's Brat Farrar." He describes the book as "a mystery novel *plus,*" one that gives "a subtly disturbing Pirandellian hint that truth may be simply what it seems to you."[3] John Bayley, in the *Spectator,* on the other hand, compares du Maurier's handling of the theme of the doppelganger with that of Henry James: "With a very similar theme in *The Sense of the Past* (except that there his doubles change places in time), Henry James was so bothered by trying to make it a novel that he gave it up, after just succeeding, in two or three hundred resonant pages, in establishing the strange *fact* of the double—a fact that Miss du Maurier knocks down smartly in a few lines."[4]

Besides Hope, Tey, and James, there are a few other authors who may have helped du Maurier to shape her theme. Robert Louis Stevenson's *The Strange Case of Dr. Jekyll and Mr. Hyde,* Mark Twain's *The Prince and the Pauper,* Joseph Conrad's *The Secret Sharer,* and Graham Greene's *The Man Within* all focus upon the idea of the double. Du Maurier tries to combine the excitement and adventure of a masquerade found in novels like *The Prisoner of Zenda* and *The Prince and the Pauper* with the more heady psychological analyses of works like *The Secret Sharer* and *The Man Within.*

Du Maurier seems to adopt an ambiguous attitude towards the duality of her hero. Jean de Gué is clearly a villain, dedicated to gratifying his own senses. He has had a man murdered, thereby turning his sister into a bitter, hateful person. He shows no compassion for the workers in his factory, which he has allowed to go bankrupt. He supports his mother's drug addiction, commits adultery with his brother's wife and with Béla, and holds little feeling for his pregnant wife. Sensuous, selfish, and violent, Jean is made out to be a Mr. Hyde figure, an irresponsible, animal self clamoring to arise from the depths of John's subconscious mind. When Jean assumes John's position, however, all he manages to do is to resign from the university,

spend his money, and sell his apartment. The fact of the matter is
that this Mr. Hyde has already done all of his serious damage in the
past, before he met John in Le Mans. It is somewhat surprising,
therefore, to hear Béla tell John that Jean is not a devil, but simply
an ordinary man.

Du Maurier's psychological portrait appears confused and confusing
when compared to characters like Stevenson's Mr. Hyde and Conrad's
Leggatt. Du Maurier's real concern is with John's involvement with
his week-long family, with his powers of healing and compassion, and
with his great discovery that love and tenderness, not greed and selfishness, give life its meaning. Du Maurier may have dabbled in the
works of Carl Jung and been familiar with his idea of the anima, an
individual's true inner self embodying archetypal desires, but the actual theme of her novel is best stated in her essay "This I Believe":
"Kindness seems to me the one quality worth praising, but today I
give it a longer word and call it compassion."[5]

John's relationship with Jean seems superficial and accidental rather
than fundamental and predestined. There never appears to be a "man
within" John after all. They have nothing in common except their
looks, a piece of good luck that allows John to share Jean's bizarre
family for a brief period. When Jean returns at the end of the novel,
he is not so much a psychological manifestation of John's alter ego as
he is a mere spoiler of John's fun in performing good deeds that must
now live on as "tendresse." Although Béla says that henceforth she
will look for John in Jean, rather than for Jean in John, du Maurier
fails to establish the Frenchman's potential for goodness. Shortly before he releases John from gunpoint, he gives a cynical caricature of
each member of his famiy and then heads off to his chateau. There is
every reason to believe that he will soon restore the enmity, bankruptcy, and moral decay of his family.

The most interesting character in the novel is Jean's neglected
daughter, Marie-Noel. Reviewers expressed differing views about this
puzzling innocent. A writer in *Time* glibly describes her as having "a
bad outbreak of mystical acne."[6] The *Times Literary Supplement* finds
her to be "charming and . . . convincingly devout."[7] Anthony Boucher, in the *New York Times Book Review,* sees her as possessing the
"startling symptoms of being a child-saint."[8] Such views, however,
seriously misrepresent du Maurier's hostile attitude towards organized
religion, which she expresses through the relationship between
Blanche and Marie-Noel.

The character of Marie-Noel is partially drawn after du Maurier's maternal grandmother. Du Maurier describes her as the "only one person in my life whom I would truly call good, . . . a little woman of great simplicity and charm. . . . I remember watching her bowed head, her closed eyes, and the fervent movement of her lips as she murmured the words of the Confession at Morning Service, and the sight of such humility filled me with outrage against the vicar, against God, that both should deem it necessary for someone as gentle and as unselfish as my little grandmother to admit to uncommitted sin." "As for sin," she goes on, "the word was meaningless. It is so still. The only sin then, as now, is cruelty, and today I know that cruelty is bred from ignorance out of fear."[9]

Marie-Noel is not a saint in du Maurier's eyes, but rather an innocent child who has been corrupted by her sexually repressed and sadomasochistic aunt. Blanche instills in her an obsession with guilt and a desire for punishment. John warns the young girl: "You know, little one, the ways of women are mysterious, especially one who is religious like your aunt. Remember that, and don't turn into a fanatic like her" (130). Marie-Noel, however, tells him that she sinned when she threatened to kill herself, and for her penance she lashed herself about the back and shoulders with a leather dog-whip. Her notion of sin also distorts her youthful innocence. She leaves a note for John stating her willingness to be the scapegoat for her father's evil: "The Sainte Vierge tells me you are unhappy, and are suffering now for wrong done in the past, so I am going to pray that all your sins may be visited upon me, who, being young and strong, can bear them better" (248). She disappears and is later found sleeping at the bottom of the well where the body of Duval was discovered fifteen years ago. Thus du Maurier's portrait of Marie-Noel is not that of a child saint but of a naive and charming youth whose mind and body have been tormented by what, in du Maurier's thinking, is the only sin: cruelty. In this sense, then, she is the true scapegoat of the novel. The cruelty of Jean, epitomized in his having Duval murdered, is inflicted upon Blanche, who hopelessly turns to religious fanaticism and self-hatred and who, in turn, imposes her holy masochism upon her helpless niece.

The Scapegoat was adapted by Gore Vidal for a motion picture directed by Robert Hamer. Financially involved with Alec Guinness in the production, du Maurier chose Guinness to play the roles of both Jacques (instead of Jean) de Gué and John Barrett. The film gives

John a surname, which he lacks in the novel. Bette Davis plays the Countess, Nicole Maurey plays Béla, Irene Worth plays Françoise, Pamela Brown plays Blanche, and Annabel Bartlett plays Marie-Noel. Despite some selected praise for individual acting parts, the critics did not like this film. Howard Thompson, in the *New York Times Film Review,* complains that "du Maurier's dazzlingly cunning puzzler is now a stately charade—handsome, curious and untingling." He can find none of the novel's causes and motivations in the film: "Why would a practical man, however lonely, assume responsibility for such oddballs?"[10] The general consensus is that Gore Vidal produced a script that failed to give adequate motivation to the characters, thereby leaving the audience confused about who was doing what to whom and for what reason. To make matters even worse, the film builds to a trick ending. Unlike the novel, the screenplay has Jean murder his wife in order to get the money from her will. He admits he killed her and announces his intention of resuming his former life. John refuses to relinquish his new life, and the two men quarrel, draw pistols, and fire. The survivor emerges from the scene to continue living as Jacques de Gué. The audience, of course, is left to speculate who the survivor actually is. The critics unanimously attacked the gratuitous confusion of this gimmicky ending.

The Glass-Blowers

Having written the biography of her father, du Maurier now traces her roots back to an eighteenth-century French family of glassblowers named Busson. The patriarch of the clan, old Mathurin Busson, is a master glassblower whose finest hour came when Louis XV took time out from one of his hunting excursions to visit him and inspect his workrooms. For the occasion Mathurin creates a crystal goblet in honor of the king and later remarks to his family: "I suggest we preserve this goblet as a family symbol, and if it does not bring us fame and fortune it shall serve as a reminder of high craftsmanship through succeeding generations."[11]

There are five children in the Busson family. Robert, the eldest, is hopelessly irresponsible and leads the family business to the brink of bankruptcy. His character resembles that of the Comte du Gué in *The Scapegoat,* who similarly allowed his glassblowing business to suffer while he enjoyed a reckless and hedonistic life. Pierre, the next oldest, is an idealist, dedicated to the principles of Rousseau. Michel, handicapped by a stammer that prevents him from communicating his emotions, becomes a fanatic who expresses his feelings through violence. Edmé, the youngest member of the family, is a sexless female who devotes her energy to seeking happiness and equality for all people by philosophicaly attacking established institutions. Finally, there is Sophie, the narrator of the story, who adopts a comfortable middle ground as she records the life of her unusual family.

Set during the French Revolution and the civil war that followed, this fictional history of the Busson family appears to have two objectives, one public and one personal. For her millions of faithful readers du Maurier combines a smattering of history, biography, and political philosophy in order to come up with an entertaining and informative historical romance. Compared with a novel like Dickens's *A Tale of Two Cities,* however, du Maurier's story seems lacking in believable, rounded characters, in rich historical detail, and in philosophic perspective. Her real interest seems to lie, not in the revolution or its philosophical underpinings, but in the life of the Busson family. Against a backdrop of melodramatic action and ideological speeches about the values of the common people du Maurier formulates the story of her family history. Believing that her ancestors contributed to the shaping of her personality, du Maurier's "historical romance" is actually a form of autobiography, a dramatization of her roots. It is this inner story, rather than the surface one, that absorbs her interest, for in it she can discover herself and recognize the truth of her favorite quotation, "In my beginning is my end."

In her essay "This I Believe" du Maurier explains her notion that her family history both shapes and is recapitulated within her personality:

As an individual living here and now I am only too well aware that I possess feelings, emotions, a mind and body bequeathed to me by people long since dead who have made me what I am. Generations of French craftsmen of the tight-knit glass-blowing fraternity, provincial, clannish, have handed on to me a strong family sense, a wary suspicion of all who are not "us." Drawing their life and sustenance from the deep forests of Vibraye and Montmirail, they have made me to their pattern, and thus, inevitably, it seemed, I sought wooded shelter, the protection of great trees, for what ultimately came to be my home. Respect for tradition vies in me with a contempt for authority imposed from above, a legacy of French temperament passed on from that nation of individualists. [12]

The central theme of this novel is precisely the same as that of her last novel, *Rule Britannia,* namely, the traditions of the past must be maintained at all costs. Although du Maurier is sympathetic towards the characters of Pierre, Michel, and Edmé, idealists who rebel against the oppressive rule of the aristocracy and clergy, she makes it quite clear that their envisioned world of equality and freedom for all cannot be purchased at the price of destroying the institutions and traditions of France. As Sophie points out by 1894 "the poor were still poor, and those who had enriched themselves by the purchase of church lands were looked upon as profiteers, despite the initial act of patriotism" (303). The workers at the glass foundry complain that they had "enough of the revolution, enough of fighting and restrictions, enough of change. It was better, so the older ones say, when [Sophie's] mother was in charge here and everyone felt settled. Now, nobody knows what tomorrow will bring" (305). After her mother dies Sophie discovers a closet full of very old linen that her mother had embroidered with great artistry many years ago, causing her to reflect: "These things, so unexpected and incongruous in our troublous times, were an indictment of our age that reverenced nothing past and hated all things old" (312).

Sophie is the survivor in this novel. Although she loves the radical Pierre, Michel and Edmé, and the irresponsible Robert, she is the only child to inherit her mother's great common sense. When her father died, it was her mother who took charge of the glass factory. She ran the business efficiently and won the respect of all the workers for her compassion and fairness in dealing with their problems. Like the idealized mother figure in *Rule Britannia,* she is a tough-minded defender of traditional values who is willing literally to go to battle for her beliefs. "If any black-faced vagrants show their faces in this neighbourhood, they will get more than they bargained for" (163), she says. Sophie sees her looking at a pitchfork leaning against the barn and thinks, "I believe she would have faced an army with this weapon, turning it from her door armed with the fork only, and her own determination" (163). Later, during the height of the revolution, Sophie asks her mother if she is opposed to the rebellion. "I'm against nothing that benefits honest people," she replies. "If a man wishes to get on in his life, he should be encouraged to do so. I don't see what that has to do with revolution. Your father became a rich man through his own efforts. He began at the bottom, like any apprentice boy" (247).

Sophie and her mother comprise the still point in the turning world of this novel. The other characters fly off in different directions and are destroyed through their reckless disregard of tradition. After the revolution Michel becomes a manager of a small glass foundry, and Edmé keeps house for him. He gambled on a dream and lost. The common bronchial disease of glassblowers finally ends his miserable life. Edmé is left with no family, no children, just the memories of her fiery revolutionary rhetoric. Pierre's devotion to the high-minded principles of Rousseau helped to bring about the death of his own child, who was killed during a skirmish in one of the civil wars, and he spends his later years managing a school for runaway children. He dies some years later attempting to save a drowning dog.

Du Maurier spends an entire chapter discussing Robert, the eldest son, who had immigrated to England for thirteen years in order to avoid the violence of the revolution at home. Having abandoned his wife and child in France, he married again in London, had six children, and was imprisoned for debt. When released from prison, he abandoned his young wife and children and returned to France. Despite his cowardice and his miserable treatment of his two families, he becomes reconciled with his brothers and sisters. In fact, he works for several years as a teacher in Pierre's school. Sophie sees the two men as perfect educators: "Pierre had the ideals and the selflessness to put those ideas into practice. Robert the powers of persuasion, the necessary charm and inventive ability to turn a history lesson into an adventure" (370). At one point Robert considered returning to England to bring his family to France, but Pierre warned him that there were threats of a French invasion across the Channel, and he abandoned the idea. He continued to work at the school for nearly seven years, never saw his children again, and finally died of a heart attack.

One reason that du Maurier presented Robert in a sympathic light, despite his abominable selfishness, is the fact that he is her great-great-grandfather. One of his sons was George du Maurier, the father of Gerald. Having created a mythical aristocratic past for himself, Robert added the "du Maurier" to his name after the name of his birthplace, the farmhouse Maurier. Daphne du Maurier makes allowances for this blackguard not only because she is descended from him but because she sees in him a powerful imaginative force. He creates his own persona, like a great actor or novelist, and it is from him that she derives her ability as a writer, her inclination to dream. Sophie, and especially Sophie's mother, on the other hand, have passed on the near sacred value of tradition and the supreme importance of a sense of family unity and stability. From Pierre, Michel, and Edmé du Maurier inherits her youthful rebellious spirit and her profound desire for freedom from arbitrary restraints. Louis Mathurin's glass goblet, the symbol of the Busson family and the symbol of tradition, winds up in the possession of Sophie who, like her creator, handles it with great care.

The Flight of the Falcon

Du Maurier's continued success at writing best-selling novels became over the years a nagging annoyance among several of her critics. Thus, the publication of *The Flight of the Falcon* afforded Patricia MacManus, writing in *Book Week*, the opportunity to attack her good fortune: "There are always customers for brand names, no matter the product; thus, Daphne du Maurier—a front-rank brand name in the popular fiction field—has come up with yet another bestseller in a little fire-sale item called *The Flight of the Falcon*."[13] *The New Yorker* gives the novel a one-sentence summary review, opening with the phrase, "This extraordinarily dull book."[14]

It is difficult to understand why the critics fell for the superficial psychology of a basically conventional, sentimental novel like *The Scapegoat* and chose to ignore the complex and compelling study of a demonic mind and of an insane quest for power and sexual domination in *The Flight of the Falcon*. The texture of this novel is that of a nightmare, and the coincidences that move the plot forward are the frightening and inexplicable coincidences we all experience in dreams.

The narrator is Armino Fabbio, a tour guide for English and American visitors in Italy. During a stopover in Rome Fabbio gives some money to an old woman sleeping in the street and experiences an overwhelming sense of déjà vu: "Once again I was seized with that sense of recognition, that link with the past which could not be explained."[15] He imagines he hears her calling after him, "Beo, Beo," the name given him as a child by his parents and by his nurse, Marta. He continues to reflect upon his childhood and his brother Aldo, who held a theory that Christ and the devil were one and the same. Like the Christ-devil, Aldo used to appear robed in a towel like Jesus, smiling, feeding Fabbio sweets, embracing him with kindness and love. At other times, however, Aldo wore the dark shirt of the Fascist Youth organizations to which he belonged, and, armed with a

kitchen fork, he would represent Satan and jab at his brother with
the weapon. Later in the novel, we see the mature Aldo playing the
same paradoxical role as savior and destroyer.

Aldo is also identified with Claudio, the mad fifteenth-century
duke named the Falcon, who in a frenzy had thrown himself from the
tower of the ducal palace at Ruffano, believing himself, so the story
ran, the Son of God. Aldo explains to his brother how the Falcon ex-
tended his arms and flew like a bird over the city. Armino argues that
he was a mere man and fell to his death, but his brother steadfastly
holds to the myth. This exchange between the brothers foreshadows
the conclusion of the novel where Aldo attempts to recreate the Falcon's magnificent flight over Ruffano.

The story shifts back to the present as Fabbio reads in the newspaper the next day that the body of a woman was found on the steps of
a church. She was stabbed to death. He feels guilty, thinking that if
he had not given her the money she would never have been murdered.
He intensifies his guilt by believing that the vagrant was none other
than Marta, whom he had not seen in twenty years. The woman's
death and his assumed involvement in it cause Fabbio to abandon his
duties as a tour guide and return to Ruffano, the place of his birth,
so that he can come to grips with his past.

Over the next few weeks Fabbio discovers that the place of his
childhood dreams has become a nightmarish world. He sees once
again above the entrance to the ducal palace the great bronze figure
of the Falcon. Memories come flooding back. He recalls how his
mother took a German officer as her lover during the occupation after
his father died of pneumonia in an Allied prison camp: "my beautiful
slut of a mother feeding her conqueror grapes" (31). Later she lived
for two years with an American officer in Frankfurt, after which she
married a banker named Enrico Fabbio. Armino then remembers stories about Aldo's death, how when he was a pilot in the war he was
shot down in flames. And he recalls the death of his mother in 1956
from cancer of the uterus. Du Maurier's brief portrait of Fabbio's
mother is one of her recurrent figures of the non-nurturing, sexually
self-indulgent woman who meets an untimely or painful death. The
cancers of both Fabbio's mother and Rebecca seem designed as pun-
ishments for their lascivious behavior.

Fabbio meets Carla Raspa, a lecturer at the university (Ruffano is
a fictional university town). She lives up to her name: "hard as nails,
with a soft centre, like a Neapolitan ice" (52). She gets him a job at

the library where he begins to research his family history. The novel takes on the form of a mystery as Fabbio attempts to unravel the threads of his past. He learns that his brother was baptized twice, a puzzling detail later cleared up when he discovers that his parents had another child who died and that they then got Aldo from a foundling home. We also find out later in the novel that Marta was Aldo's actual mother and that the reason Marta left Ruffano was that she had gotten into a heated argument with Aldo and told him that he was a foundling and her son. He felt so disgraced by this news that he drove her away, and she became an alcoholic, winding up on the street where Fabbio saw her and gave her the money.

Carla brings Fabbio to a secret meeting of the arts students at which Aldo, in a torchlight setting, proclaims the story of Claudio, the Falcon. Like Claudio, who surrounded himself with a small band of dissolute disciples, Aldo establishes an elite corps of students who appreciate art and enforce their cultural superiority with violent methods. The festival, Aldo announces, will this year reenact the "uprising of the city of Ruffano against their much misunderstood lord and master, Claudio" (90). Although his pitch to the arts students is that they are the elite, Aldo later addresses a huge crowd of commerce and education students and convinces them that as "the people" they are the most important segment of society and should overthrow the elite. He warns them that a small clique is out to do them in and that the forthcoming event, in order to be authentic, may be dangerous. They should, therefore, be armed with the appropriate historical weapons.

Hearing his brother's rhetoric and witnessing his hypnotic control over his audience, Fabbio recalls Aldo's powerful and manipulative presence when he was a young boy: "This was the same power, but maturer, dangerous" (92). Some of the students view the charismatic Aldo as a communist, some as a fascist, and others simply as a magnificent hoaxer. Aldo enjoys not only controlling the crowds of students around him but takes especial delight in dominating beautiful young women. Sickened at the thought that a low-class woman like Marta should be his mother, Aldo became cynical towards women in general and used them simply to satisfy his lust for power and his hatred for Marta. He now enjoys an affair with Professor Butali's wife while her husband is in the hospital.

Comparing himself to Lazarus, Fabbio finally reveals himself to his brother. Aldo, another Lazarus figure, explains to Fabbio how he escaped from the burning airplane during the war. The plane was climbing when it was hit. "The explosion and my release in the sky happened almost simultaneously, and the moment of triumph, of ecstasy, was indescribable. It was death and it was power. Creation and destruction all in one. I had lived and I had died" (120). Aldo's language reveals the nature of his pathological mind: he needs an intense excitement that brings him close to death in order to experience the sense of creation. The festival will thus allow him to project his madness on the grand scale of a pageant.

Illusion and reality, fiction and fact, begin to blend together as the novel progresses. Aldo chooses to follow the scenario of the duke's final days as set forth in a German scholar's historical account of Claudio. Before the uprising there must be "the seduction of the lady." Reports soon circulate among the students that Signorina Rizzio, the old-maid sister of the Deputy-Rector and Head of the Department of Education, has been raped. Carla Raspa takes great pleasure in this gossip: "You have to hand it to those C and E boys. Imagine the nerve." Then she asks Fabbio, "Do you suppose she enjoyed it?" (137). Seeing the sadistic gleam in her eyes, Fabbio begins to feel sick and concludes that his brother must have planned this rape to stir the confrontation between the elite and the masses.

Fabbio studies the painting "Temptation of Christ" hanging in the duke's bedroom. The face of Christ bears the likeness of Claudio, and the tempter, Satan, "was the same Christ in profile, suggesting, not a lack of models, but a rash attempt at truth" (182). This scene is foreshadowed earlier in the novel when Fabbio remembers his brother as a boy adopting the roles of both Christ and Satan. Fabbio concludes that his brother has gone insane after he hears him paraphrase Jesus: "I'm here to bring trouble and discord, to set one man against the other, to bring all the violence and hypocrisy and envy and lust out into the open, on to the surface" (193).

On the day of the festival Aldo and his brother drive their chariot, pulled by eighteen horses, through the city to commemorate the duke's mad flight from the people. No battle among the people, however, takes place, for the wild ride of the Falcon unites the two groups of students. Aldo explains that this was his real plan, one that involved his gambling with hundreds of lives. He then climbs the tower of the ducal palace and puts on a great pair of wings and launches himself into the air to fly, like the Falcon, over the heads of his people. Fabbio describes the suicidal flight:

I watched for him to pull the rip-cord of the breaking parachute, as he had described. He did not do so. Instead, he must have kicked his body free, letting the apparatus which he had helped to build drift on without him. He threw himself clear, spreading his arms wide like the wings he had discarded, then, bringing them to his side, he plummeted to earth and fell, his body, small and fragile, a black streak against the sky. (270)

The novel concludes with an extract from the Ruffano newspaper, written by Professor Butali, acknowledging Aldo Donati's greatness. Butali also reports that Fabbio, who will probably work with orphaned students at Ruffano (his brother's disciples were mostly orphans), said that his brother "in mid air, had a sudden vision, some sort of ecstasy blinding him to danger. It may be true. Like Icarus, he flew too near the sun. Like Lucifer, he fell" (272).

Like George du Maurier's Svengali, Aldo has become a dangerous sexual psychopath who asserts his dominance over both men and women. Fabbio confesses that his life became empty after his brother's "death," and, despite his recognition of Aldo's insanity, he continues to romanticize him, praising him for daring to carry out his mad flight over the people. Aldo is a grotesque parody of the desires of romantic poets like Shelley and Byron, with their longings for unbridled freedom and ecstasy in a finite world that begrudges their dreams. Du Maurier's own rebellious spirit can also be glimpsed in her sympathetic portrayal of this Svengali-Icarus figure. Like her father, Aldo is a great actor, the tragic hero of his own drama, and du Maurier, like Aldo's younger brother, stands in awe at his performance. Seductive and domineering, he brings fiction to life with all of Ruffano as his stage, and his identification with and recreation of a mythic hero leads to his destruction. He destroys himself in the act of creation.

This novel also explores the theme of lost innocence. Fabbio returns to Ruffano hoping to discover his roots and thereby come to a firmer understanding of who he is. The simplicity of his childhood memories, however, is displaced by the tension, scandals, and violence of Aldo's Ruffano. Fabbio's world has been reshaped by his malevolent brother into an incomprehensible nightmare. The more knowledge he acquires the further removed he becomes from his childhood. Nevertheless, despite the murder of Marta, the rape of Signorina Rizzio, the sexual advances of the sadistic Carla Raspa, Aldo's affair with Professor Butali's wife, and the complex intrigues involved in the festival, Fabbio manages to maintain his hero worship of his brother. In choosing to work with orphaned students after his brother's death, he acknowledges both the suffering of Aldo and his own need to help heal the great wounds inflicted upon his memory.

The clue to reading this novel may be found in du Maurier's essay "This I Believe." Dispensing with the conventional tenets of Christianity, du Maurier explains that when Jesus said "The Kingdom of God is within you" he meant just that. Divinity is another name for the "sixth sense," "an indefinable grasp of things unknown," an inner power that can release the full potential of a person. To du Maurier, Aldo Donati, like Jesus or Prometheus, dares to refashion men "by breathing fire upon them, to turn them from figures of clay and matter into living gods."[16] She adopts the romantic notion of Robert Browning that it is more glorious for a person to fail in his striving after unattainable goals than it is for him to attain lowly ones. Writing of Jesus and Prometheus, du Maurier says, "Their failure was their glory. For only by daring can man evolve, shake himself free, triumph over the hereditary shackles that bind him to his own species. Only by daring can the spirit, hitherto a prisoner in matter, break away from the body's ties, travel at will across time and space . . . and venture into the unknown, untrammelled, free."[17]

Whether Lucifer or Jesus, destroyer or savior, Aldo is a revolutionary who breathes new life into Ruffano. Like Jesus, Lucifer, and Icarus, he challenges the status quo and is forced to suffer for his daring. It is difficult for readers who have come to see this author as Dame du Maurier, distinguished and genteel author, to accept the fact that she is at times startlingly unconventional. Incest, murder, rape, and assorted cruelties abound in her writings. It should come as no surprise that someone like Aldo Donati, a hater of women, a violent and sexually disturbed egomaniac, should be among du Maurier's sympathetic heroes. Professor Butali's statemement, the last sentence of the novel, echoes du Maurier's own observation quoted above: "We, the Ruffanesi who remain, salute the courage of a man who dared" (272). Butali's article, interestingly enough, appeared during Easter Week, suggesting the rebirth of Aldo's powerful spirit among his followers.

The House on the Strand

Du Maurier believed that extrasensory perception, precognition, telepathy, and "dreaming true" are all aspects of the unconscious mind or, as she calls it, "the sixth sense." The following passage, in which she argues that the unconscious mind may be the panacea for society's ills, might have served as an introduction to her novel *The House on the Strand:*

This untapped source of power, this strange and sometimes mystical intuitive sense, may come to be, generations hence, mankind's salvation. If we can communicate, one with another, by thought alone, if a message from the storehouse can act as a panacea to pain, so curing the body's suffering, if recognition of a fault, a crime, can be understood before it is committed, if dreaming in time can recapture from the past certain events known to our forebears but unperceived by us, then surely a series of possibilities, multitudinous, astonishing, may lie ahead for our children's children.[18]

Experiments with hallucinogens during the 1960s interested du Maurier, for she saw in them a possibility for exploring and tapping the unknown powers of the unconscious. In *The House on the Strand* she blends the current fascination with mind-altering "trips" with her own obsession with the past to create an up-to-date romantic thriller.

For years writers have toyed with the notion that time is a continuum, that the past and future have a reality coexistent with the present, and that given the proper means one can travel that continuum. Charles Dickens's *A Christmas Carol,* Mark Twain's *A Connecticut Yankee in King Arthur's Court* and H. G. Wells's *The Time Machine* are perhaps the best-known accounts of time travel. George du Maurier's *Peter Ibbetson,* however, is Daphne du Maurier's most likely inspiration for *The House on the Strand.* The hero of *Peter Ibbetson* learns the art of "dreaming true," whereby he is able to travel back to his childhood where, invisible and inaudible, he can watch himself and his family. Later he discovers that he can travel back even further in time, all the way to prehistoric times. He cannot, of course, affect events in the past but merely witness them, sometimes with a nostalgia that is excruciatingly painful. Like her grandfather, du Maurier has an obsession with the past that makes it as vivid and real to her as the present, and the hero of her novel is the embodiment of that obsession.

The setting for the story is Kilmarth, du Maurier's own six-hundred-year-old house (in which she still lives) in Cornwall. The narrator, Dick Young, has been lent this house by his friend, Magnus Lane, a professor of biophysics. Dick has agreed while there to act as a guinea pig for a new drug that Magnus has discovered. Not knowing the effect of the drug, he swallows the liquid and finds himself back in the fourteenth century, in the same Cornish countryside. In the days that follow he takes several more "trips," each one lasting only a short time. He always finds himself in the same surroundings but usually several years later in the fourteenth century. Invisible and inaudible, he is told by Lane never to touch anyone. He soon discovers that he is a sort of alter ego of Roger Kylmerth, steward to Sir Henry Champernoune, lord of the manor of Tywardreath. With Roger as his contact point in the past, Dick witnesses murder, political intrigue, and adultery; becomes personally involved in the lives of the people of that era; and falls in love with a beautiful young woman named Isolda.

Du Maurier's distaste for Americans surfaces through her portrayal of Dick's wife, Vita. Her name is ironic because the life her husband seeks lies away from her, deep in the past. She and her American relatives are depicted as shallow, vulgar, and boring, caring only for the material comforts of the present. Vita urges Dick to accept a job in a New York publishing firm run by her brother, but he resists the offer, wanting to remain in England in order to follow his medieval dream vision, Isolda. In a way, this novel reverses the fantasy situation in *Frenchman's Creek,* where Dona seeks to escape her dull husband through an adventure with a pirate, by featuring a husband who plunges into the past to enjoy a vicarious romance. Dick says of Vita, "I was dead to her world,"[19] and as his love grows for Isolda he loses all sexual interest in Vita.

As Dick becomes more deeply enmeshed in his private world he loses the fine distinction between illusion and reality: "The people I had seen were not shadows from my own past. Roger the steward was not my alter-ego, nor Isolda a dream-fantasy, a might-have-been. Or were they?" (95). When Isolda falls in love with Otto Bodrugan, a gallant rebel against the king (reminiscent of Richard Grenvile), Dick expresses a curious response to their lovemaking: "They held each other, kissing, and once again I felt this strange disturbance, a sense of loss, utterly unlike anything I might experience in my own time, had I seen two lovers from a window. . . . Intense involvement, and intense compassion too. Yes, that was the word, compassion" (144).

Dick resembles a man enjoying the fruits of his mid-life crisis. His dull life with a middle-class, ambitious wife and two children offers him no hope, and his awareness of the shortness of life makes his fantasy affair all that more intense. A voyeur looking through the peephole of several centuries, he says, "And I had no way of explaining my sense of participation in all they [Isolda and Otto] did, unless it was that stepping backwards, out of my time to theirs, I felt them vulnerable, and more certainly doomed to die than I was myself, knowing indeed that they had both been dust for more than six centuries" (144). This bizarre parable of adultery is further adduced from Vita's reading a letter to her husband from Magnus saying that he hopes Dick's girl shows up. Knowing that Vita assumes he is having an affair, Dick thinks, with masterful understatement, "My innocence would be difficult to prove" (152).

Dick's speculation on the significance of his time travels sets forth du Maurier's central theme that time is a continuum:

Roger was my keeper, I was his. There was no past, no present, no future. Everything living is part of the whole. We are all bound, one to the other, through time and eternity, and, our senses once opened, as mine had been opened by the drug, to a new understanding of his world and mine, fusion would take place, there would be no separation, there would be no death. (202–3)

It would be a mistake, however, to consider Dick's thoughts about time and identity as du Maurier's serious reflections on the nature of man. What du Maurier seems to be doing here is commenting on the act of reading itself. Like her narrator, Dick, the reader of this novel identifies with the hero, enters his world, and shares his feelings and thoughts. Similarly, Dick enters the fictional world of medieval Cornwall and identifies with Roger Kylmerth. Roger is described as playing "Virgil to our Dante in this particular Inferno. . . . there's no escaping him" (24).

Furthermore, this novel asserts the romantic notion that fiction can alter reality. Dreaming of Isolda, Dick makes passionate love to Vita, confusing the two women. She praises him for his vigorous lovemaking, but he thinks to himself, "The towel, wrapped turban-fashion round her head, and the mask of cream gave her a clown-like appearance, and suddenly I felt revolted by the puppet world in which I found myself, and desired to be no part of it, neither now, nor tomorrow, nor at any time. I wanted to vomit" (274). He then goes off to sleep by himself in another room. Consumed by the "fiction" of the past, he can no longer tolerate the present.

Dick's physician urges him to take his family to a vacation in Ireland. After he gets his wife and children on the plane Dick sneaks off in order to take a final trip into the past. Using the last of Magnus's drug, he returns to medieval Cornwall, but this time he arrives at a point in time when Isolda and most of the other people whom he knew are dead. "This was not the world I knew," he thinks, "the world I had come to love and long for because of its magic quality of love and hate, its separation from a drab monotony; this was a place resembling, in its barren desolation, all the most hideous features of a twentieth-century landscape after disaster, suggesting a total abandonment of hope, the aftertaste of atomic doom" (343). The black plague had swept the land. Roger, Dick's alter ego, is white-haired, gaunt, obviously suffering from the illness. He feels responsible for Isolda's death because he allowed her to die in her sleep rather than leave the house and enter the devasted world. "I gave her something to ease pain," he says, "and let her slip away. . . . It was murder and a mortal sin" (346).

Dick leaves the past once and for all, returns to Magnus's house, and receives a phone call from his wife in Ireland. As he picks up the receiver his hand goes numb, and the phone crashes to the floor. With that, the novel ends. Each time Dick has taken the drug he suffered some debilitation, and the final side effect is total paralysis and, presumably, death. Dick's parallel life with Roger is thus complete: both men, having lost their Isolda, their dream vision, find themselves in a barren world facing death.

Rule Britannia

Du Maurier's last novel, *Rule Britannia,* is her testament to the traditional values of English culture and character and to the fierce spirit of independence and patriotism of the people of Cornwall. Her longstanding anti-Americanism comes full bloom here as she depicts the United States as a materialistic, ruthless, barbarian power that dares to invade the sanctuary of Western culture. Although set in Cornwall some few years in the future (Elizabeth is still queen), the novel is not really as futuristic as it is historical. Having lived for so many years in an imaginative past and in ancient homes encrusted with history, du Maurier waxes paranoid, defending her homeland against the greedy and tasteless Americans who would turn all of Cornwall into a tourist attraction that would rival Disneyland.

In the future world of this novel England's participation in the Common Market has failed. Prices have risen nearly fifty percent, and a general election reveals the country to be divided about what course of action to take. The coalition government, pressured by American financiers, prepares to accept as the solution a union of the two countries named USUK (United States United Kingdom). The acronym, when pronounced—"You suck"—reveals du Maurier's bitter satirical tone in this novel.

Suddenly the United States marines land off the coast of Cornwall, set up roadblocks, issue ration cards, and maintain a warship offshore and helicopters overhead. The American Revolution has been reversed as the country folk of Cornwall rise in unison to face the invaders. Radio and television report that Queen Elizabeth is on the way to the White House to become co-President of USUK. The Cornish people do not like the talk of a new currency or American bureaucrats prying into their activities. They reject the Madison Avenue notion that Britain can become the playground of the Americas, a new Williamsburg for wealthy American tourists.

The leader of the resistance is a seventy-nine-year-old retired actress known affectionately as Madam, or, to her granddaughter, as "Mad." Retired to the small fishing village of Poldrea, Mad lives with her six adopted boys, ranging in age from nineteen to three, her twenty-one-year-old granddaughter, Emma, and her dresser for forty years, Dottie. Edward Weeks describes Mad as "an admirable character, her courage and resourcefulness equal to any provocation, who dresses in costume, part Robin Hood and part Mao Tse-tung. She is the spirit of Britannia."[20] When a marine fires the first shot, which kills her neighbor's sheepdog, her opposition is implacable. She goes on the warpath, and, with the assistance of her neighbor, Jack Trembath, she organizes a sit-down movement that gradually spreads throughout Cornwall and later throughout the United Kingdom. Her fierce determination is in part sponsored by the fact that she has to cover up for one of her boys who killed a marine with his bow and arrow. Thanks to Mad's single-minded resistance, the Americans finally retreat on her eightieth birthday, and the novel ends with the American helicopters racing eastward into the sun.

The character of Mad represents many of the virtues of womanhood that du Maurier instilled in her earlier heroines. She is independent, rebellious, courageous, quick-witted, and domineering. Besides having enjoyed a full professional life as an actress, she managed to raise a son (who has become a financier who supports USUK), and in her retirement she still has enough maternal care and energy to adopt and nurture six boys. Critical of grandmother's dominance, Emma observes that "Mad was the last person in the world who should be permitted to give a home to maladjusted children. Happy they might be, but the world they lived in was unreal, a world of fantasy."[21] The language here is remarkably similar to that of Maria's husband, Charles, in *The Parasites,* who condemns the three Delaneys "for living in a world of fantasy which you have created for yourselves and which bears no relation to anything in heaven or on earth."[22] The recurrent theme apparently derives from du Maurier's own childhood. Inspired by the professional role playing of her actor-father, she created a rich fantasy life for herself. More important, of course, the greater part of du Maurier's professional life was given over to the fantasy worlds of her fiction. It is quite clear in both *The Parasites* and this novel that neither Charles's nor Emma's criticism is taken seriously by the author herself. She treats both of her dreamers, Maria and Mad, with the utmost sympathy.

Unlike Emma, who is young and interested in the handsome American soldiers, Mad can find no saving grace in the American presence. She is supported in her rebellion by a mysterious Welsh beachcomber named Willis. Seventy-years old and intensely loyal to his British heritage, he performs most of Mad's dirty work. When one of Mad's boys kills an American soldier, Willis disposes of the body.

Despite the satiric tone of the novel, du Maurier's bitterness towards the Americans sometimes overwhelms the narrative, as it does, for example, in her description of the death and disposal of the young marine. "The arrow's jagged tip," she writes, "must have pierced some vital point behind the corporal's right eye, because part of the eye lolled out, horribly, and the blood that had flowed at first was now congealed" (123). Willis carries the body off, and, in order to disguise the arrow wound in the head, he smashes the face of the corpse into pieces and hurls the body into the sea. With typical British understatement he tells Mad, "Had to smash his head a bit more before putting him in the water, and the sea will do the rest" (158). The young boy who killed the marine laments the fact that his father is not alive: "A boy likes his father to know when he's made his first kill" (138). Du Maurier appears to take a genuine delight in these ghoulish descriptions and sentiments.

The morality in this book is a curious one. Du Maurier suggests that Mad and her children may kill American soldiers with impunity even, as in the case of the corporal, when they are just innocently approaching their house. The notion here seems to be that since Mad sees the American presence as an invasion, she is justified in taking whatever actions she deems appropriate to protect her territory. Emma, du Maurier's pro forma critic and foil to Mad, blames her grandmother for the murder: "She had encouraged fantasy, built up their imaginations, and this, for Andy certainly, had now proved his undoing. How could a child tell truth from falsehood, reality from make-believe, when she who had nurtured him from babyhood had fed him with images of her own creation, phantoms from a grease-paint world?" (125). Mad justifies her boy's actions as follows: "If, as a small child you are the sole survivor of an aircrash, and are found lying unhurt shielded by your father's body, it has a traumatic effect. Some day you hit back. Unfortunately for the corporal, the opportunity came tonight" (131).

The satirical tone of the novel is reminiscent of Evelyn Waugh's *The Loved One.* Du Maurier focuses her humor through the character of Martha Hubbard (Mother Hubbard?), an American dispatched to Cornwall to organize the CGT ("Cultural-Get-Together"). She proposes that the west coast, from Wales to Cornwall, be developed as "one vast leisure-land." The Welsh folk would be dressed in their costumes, tall hats and cloaks, and they would serve potato cakes to the tourists from the States. The people from Cornwall would work as ski instructors and sleigh drivers in the miniature Switzerland that would be constructed out of the white mountains.

The sophisticated and stately Dame du Maurier sometimes stoops rather low to find her humor. She seems to be cheering her heroine on during Operation-Dung Cart. Mad and other villagers dump piles of cow dung by an American road block and outside of the Sea Rest, a cafe supportive of USUK. Her preoccupation with fecal humor is also illustrated in a scene with an American officer named Cheeseman and Mad's children. While the British and American anthems are being played on television, Colin, Mad's six-year-old, comes running into the room to announce that Ben, her three-year-old black son, has just spoken his first word. Cheeseman says, "I guess this is doubly an historic occasion, and I'm proud to be in on it. Come here, little fellow, and let's hear what you have to say." Ben rolls his eyes towards Colin and Colin nods his head. Ben then walks towards Cheeseman. "Sh . . .," he begins, "sh . . .," then pauses as though to summon greater strength. "Come on, son, don't be afraid," says Cheeseman, "this is the finest moment in your young life, and maybe in all of ours as well" (45). "Shit!" says Ben.

While Mad is enjoying Operation Dung-Cart, one of her boys and Willis blow up the ship in the harbor, killing and maiming over two hundred men. Mad then gives a fiery speech over Willis's secret short-wave radio encouraging all of England to rebel against USUK. If Mad represents old Britannia, then Emma stands for the uncommitted youth of England. "I'm no longer one of them," Emma thinks, "I've been cut out of it, told to mind my own business. I'm class conscious, I don't belong." Emma was "located in a sort of no-man's-land between her contemporaries and the aged" (241).

Mad's rebellion does indeed spread throughout the nation, and on her eightieth birthday the Americans pack up and leave England. Her older boys are released from military prison, and Emma sees Mad standing on the top of the porch with her arms out to greet them. They do not see her, however, only Emma does, for Mad died in her sleep the night before and Emma sees her ghost. One of the young boys comes out of the house to release his pet pigeon because he had a "feeling she wanted to be free" (318). With that rather corny symbolism, set against the helicopters flying eastward towards the sun, the novel ends.

A critic in the *Economist* writes that "too many major British novelists, who can write, seem to live in social circles which are totally divorced from any understanding of the current political or industrial scene," and he cites du Maurier as a "frightening example . . . of this divorce between the real world and the British romantics'." He notes that the character of Mad embodies "what the authoress regards as all the virtues (extreme environmentalist, gracefully patronising to the lower classes, does noble social work by adopting disturbed boys, even including an 'ebony skinned' piccaninny." After poking fun at du Maurier's attitude towards tourism and business takeovers, he goes on to mock her cavalier attitude towards the violent deaths of the Americans: "they [the Americans] are unreasonably cross when one of the disturbed boys murders one of their marines, and turn nasty like Miss du Maurier thinks they are in Vietnam." After Willis blows up two hundred marines, the critic complains, "we are supposed to cheer . . . and our cheers swell to a crescendo when the lovable Welshman announces that 'the boyos have landed'; which means that the fanciful Miss du Maurier has conscripted poor Prince Charles to land in Wales and lead what can only be called the British hick-fascist revolt."[23]

Du Maurier's romantic notion of an ideal society is articulated by several of her characters. Nineteen-year-old Joe, for example, ponders: "I believe if people formed little groups and just helped each other, became self-supporting amongst their neighbours, they could get by without having to do with the world outside at all. We'd grow our own food, burn our own fuel, use wool from our own sheep for clothes" (235). Emma echoes this same call for self reliance: "we should all live in small communities, sharing each other's work and needs . . ., but no money any more" (281). Barter is good, money is evil; homegrown vegetables are good, international trade is evil.

There will always be an England as long as there is a Mad or a Willis to reaffirm the principles of independence, superiority, and national pride. As the critic in the *Economist* observes, du Maurier, in expounding upon the theme of the decay of Britain's traditional values "writes like a major novelist even while thinking like Little Noddy."[24] Joseph Kanon, in the *Saturday Review of Arts,* points to the fundamental ambiguity in this novel: "it is difficult to tell whether this fantasy is written with irony or genteel paranoia. Is this a warning about Europeanization (America being a melodramatic metaphor), an outright 'Yankee, Go Home' pitch, or a governess telling her own charges to get cracking?"[25]

The important word in Kanon's article is "fantasy." The social, political, and economic views expressed in *Rule Britannia* are there to bolster du Maurier's vision of her past, a past she does not want to see changed. As the *Economist* points out, du Maurier is out of touch with current economic and political theories and practices. Her reclusive lifestyle has placed severe limits on her understanding of other people and other cultures. The romantic legends of Cornwall, blended with her own long and happy memories of Menabilly and Kilmarth, became her life; and in *Rule Britannia* she is defending that life the only way she knows how, by creating another fiction. In the "Mad house" of that novel she seeks to preserve not only the traditional values of Britain, but the rich memories of her own family, along with her creations of such figures as Janet Coombe, Mrs. Danvers, Mary Anne Clarke, and the dozens of other characters she fashioned over five decades.

Chapter Six
The World of the Macabre: The Short Stories

Before she embarked on her career as a novelist du Maurier had published a few of her short stories in the *Bystander*, a magazine edited by her maternal uncle, William Comyns Beaumont. She continued writing short stories during the next five decades, many of which appeared in such women's magazines as the *Ladies Home Journal* and *Good Housekeeping*. Most of these tales were later collected and published in *The Apple Tree*, 1952 (entitled *Kiss Me Again, Stranger* in the American edition), *The Breaking Point*, 1959, *Not After Midnight*, 1971 (entitled *Don't Look Now* in the American edition), and *The Rendezvous and Other Stories*, 1980. *Echoes from the Macabre*, published in 1976, is a composite of selected stories from the earlier collections. Finally, some of the stories that appeared in these earlier books are reprinted, along with a few previously uncollected essays and early tales, in *The Rebecca Notebook and Other Memories*, 1980.

Although some of du Maurier's novels, such as *The House on the Strand* and *The Flight of the Falcon*, acknowledge the workings of the unconscious mind, most of her short stories focus upon this sixth sense and explore the region of the mind that borders upon reason and madness, the natural and the supernatural. In her preface to *The Breaking Point*, du Maurier writes, "There comes a moment in the life of every individual when reality must be faced. When this happens, it is as though a link between emotion and reason is stretched to the limit of endurance, and sometimes snaps."[1] Two of her tales that study this breaking point, "The Birds," and "Don't Look Now," have been indelibly etched upon millions of minds through the enormously popular films by Alfred Hitchcock and Nicholas Roeg.

"The Birds" is an excellent short story that has been turned into a very bad motion picture. "On December the third the wind changed overnight and it was winter,"[2] the story opens. This sudden shift in the weather sets the tone for the catastrophic change in the natural order of things to follow. The tale focuses upon an English farmer,

Nat Hocken, his wife and children. As the cold begins to bite into both the land and Nat's body, he notices that there are more birds than usual, both over the sea and land. That night he hears pecking at the windows of his home. The birds are trying to get in, and when he goes to investigate the noise one of them pecks at his eyes. Some fifty birds then fly through the open window in his children's room, and he manages to kill most of them amidst the hysterical cries of the children.

The next day the family discusses the bizarre occurrence. Nat explains that the east wind must have affected the behavior of the birds and caused them to seek shelter in his house. When his daughter, Jill, says that they tried to peck at her brother's eyes, Nat again offers a rational explanation. "Fright made them do that. They didn't know where they were, in the dark bedroom" (91).

Later that day, Nat sees what he thinks are white caps out at sea, but they turn out to be hundreds of thousands of gulls: "They rose and fell in the trough of the seas, heads to the wind, like a mighty fleet at anchor, waiting on the tide" (95). When he returns home his wife informs him that there was an announcement on the radio stating that "it's everywhere. In London, all over the country. Something has happened to the birds" (95). A later bulletin says that "The flocks of birds have caused dislocation in all areas" (97).

"Dislocation" is a key word in this story, for it identifies the fundamental disruption in the natural order of things. Man, who is ordained to have dominion over the birds and the beasts, suddenly has his authority threatened. There is not only a dislocation in the great chain of being but within people's minds. Reason and serenity are displaced by fear and panic in this unexpected reversion to a Darwinian world of the survival of the fittest.

Realizing that neither the government nor the military could do anything to help at this point, Nat assumes the thinking of a survivalist: "Each householder must look after his own" (98). Life within his small farmhouse takes on the character of Londoners during the air raids: the family huddles together, food is carefully accounted for, windows and other openings are sealed up, as they prepare for the invasion. The next day the birds continue to gather ominously in the sky and in the fields. On his way home Nat is viciously attacked by a gull, and during his panic a dozen other gulls join in. "If he could only keep them from his eyes. They had not learnt yet how to cling to a shoulder, how to rip clothing, how to dive in mass upon the head, upon the body. But with each dive, with each attack, they became bolder" (104).

Safe at home again, Nat has his wounds treated by his wife, and his children become terrified at the sight of the blood. The battle is now in earnest. The parents do their best to keep the children distracted, but their gut fear shows in their faces and in their actions. That night thousands of birds assault the house, breaking the windows, screaming down the chimney. Using all of his energy and resourcefulness, Nat manages to get his family through the harrowing hours. Daylight brings a degree of safety, for the birds seem to settle quietly in the fields.

Nat goes to the home of his neighbor, the Triggs, to see if he can get some food for his family and discovers the mutilated bodies of the couple. Mr. Trigg is lying next to his telephone, and his wife, an umbrella and a few dead birds at her side, is lying on her bedroom floor. Nat gathers up some food and returns home. This time he barricades his house with barbed wire around the boarded windows and chimney. He works feverishly as his wife and children sleep and then joins them in the hope that his small world is secure.

The story ends with Nat lighting up his last cigarette and listening to the attack of the birds:

The smaller birds were at the window now. He recognized the light tap-tapping of their beaks, and the soft brush of their wings. The hawks ignored the windows. They concentrated their attack upon the door. Nat listened to the tearing sound of splintering wood, and wondered how many millions of years were stored in those little brains, behind the stabbing beaks, the piercing eyes, now giving them this instinct to destroy mankind with all the deft precision of machines. (122–23)

By limiting the focus of her story upon Nat Hocken and his family du Maurier manages to convey the effect of a believable claustrophobic nightmare. The birds may be attacking people throughout the world, but du Maurier wisely keeps the story within the confines of one person's family (though, of course, Nat hears reports of the birds turning predatory in London). The Hocken family becomes a microcosm of an apparent world-wide disaster, and the conclusion of the story clearly suggests that the birds will destroy all the people on earth.

During recent years there have been stories and films featuring everything from rabbits to ants as man's final enemy. Du Maurier's story, however, was something of a shocker at the time, and her choice of birds as the destroyers was particularly effective. Birds have long been associated with peacefulness, beauty, freedom, spirituality, music, and poetry. Unlike ants, frogs, rats, bees, and the other assortments of creatures that go on the rampage in contemporary science fiction tales, birds are attractive and elusive creatures. By making them relentless, almost calculating predators, du Maurier revolutionizes the traditional symbolism of birds, and her story conjures up the nightmarish imagery of the paintings by Hieronymus Bosch, in which grotesque birds with stabbing beaks threaten the rational order of things. Du Maurier plays upon the archetypal fear of having one's eyes pierced by having Nat several times throughout the story exclaim in the midst of an attack that he must protect his eyes.

One other nice touch in the story is that du Maurier does not offer some pseudo-scientific explanation for the birds' behavior. Given an ordered and reasonable world, her characters attempt to explain the phenomena in terms they can understand—a shift in the weather or migration patterns. They gradually discover, however, that their life-long assumptions about reason and order do not apply, that their world has suddenly become absurd, a bad dream in which rules of logic and common sense no longer work. The end result is that human beings are forced to act like animals themselves, with survival as their solitary goal.

Alfred Hitchcock became interested in du Maurier's story after he read the headlines of a Santa Cruz newspaper: "A Sea Bird Invasion Hits Coastal Homes." Realizing that there was no plot or character development in the short story, Hitchcock knew he would have to get someone, preferably a novelist, who could expand the story and make it suitable for a film. He turned to the novelist Evan Hunter.

Hunter's final story line is as follows: A rich San Francisco socialite named Melanie Daniels (played by Tippi Hedren) meets a brash young lawyer named Mitch Brenner (played by Rod Taylor) in a pet shop. Despite Mitch's arrogant manner, Melanie is attracted to him, and she travels by boat to his home in Bodega Bay to deliver a pair of love birds his young sister wanted. Returning to town, Melanie is attacked by a swooping gull that wounds her head. Later she accepts an invitation to Mitch's home for dinner, despite his mother's disapproval of her. The birds in the area, meantime, show signs of erratic behavior. Melanie goes to help out at the sister's birthday party the next day, and during the party a flock of gulls attacks the children.

The school teacher, Annie Hayworth (played by Suzanne Pleshette), was formerly in love with Mitch and provides the love triangle.

The violence increases as a flock of sparrows pours into the house through the chimney. A neighboring farmer and his wife are pecked to death; another attack leads to an explosion of a gasoline tank; and Annie is killed while trying to protect her students. Finally, Melanie, Mitch, his mother and sister, barricade the house against a brutal onslaught of birds. During a lull the next day, Mitch gets his car, and he drives the terrified group away slowly down a road surrounded by birds.

Hitchcock did not want any stars in his film. He told Hunter, "I'm the star, the birds are the stars—and you're the star."[3] Apart from the famous stage actress Jessica Tandy, who played the mother, there were no well-known actors in the film. Hitchcock chose Suzanne Pleshette, a newcomer, over Anne Bancroft for the role of the schoolteacher. He gave Tippi Hedren and Rod Taylor their first leading roles. A great expense of time and money went into the birds themselves: mechanical birds, animated birds, and real birds. Two men, wearing protective gloves, threw live birds at Tippi Hedren during the climactic scene. Hours were spent in shooting this scene in a caged room as Hedren attempted to act under the constant bombardment of feathers and beaks. Once a frightened bird left a deep gash on her lower eye lid, and the terror in the cage became more than mere acting.

If a lesser figure than Hitchcock had produced this film it is doubtful that it would have received such enormous notoriety. It is without a doubt the worse film version of a du Maurier story. Evan Hunter's script is largely devoted to the dull and unbelievable love story between Mitch and Melanie. The audience must sit through over an hour of poor acting and vapid dialogue before the birds get their chance to star. The nightmare effect of du Maurier's story is diminished beyond recall, with the exception of one excellent scene in which Melanie sits outside the school house waiting for Mitch's sister. As she sits there smoking a cigarette, a jungle-gym set in the background ominously fills up with large blackbirds.

Brendal Gill, in the *New Yorker,* observes that the film "doesn't arouse suspense, which is, of course, what justifies and transforms the sadism that lies at the heart of every thriller. Here the sadism is all too nakedly, repellently present. . . . If this picture is a hit, the Audubon Society has an ugly public-relations problem on its hands."[4]

Most of the major newspapers and magazines attacked this film with the vehemence of the predatory birds themselves. Before long, the critics were busily attacking each other. Gary Arnold in *Moviegoer* ridicules the opinions of Peter Bogdanovich and Andrew Sarris, who contend that *The Birds* is Hitchcock's greatest artistic achievement. Arnold observes that Evan Hunter's script lies at the heart of the film's failure: "Since the people in the film are so shallow, so lacking in the qualities and complexities of human beings, the birds themselves lose a good deal of force both as terrorizers and possible symbols. Assaulting vacant, passive, cardboard figures proves very little, I think, about what men are like or what they may have in store for themselves."[5]

In a prefatory note to *The Breaking Point,* du Maurier writes that "In this collection of stories, men, women, children, and a nation are brought to the breaking point. Whether the link [between emotion and reason] snaps, the reader must judge for himself."[6] The two most memorable tales in this volume are "The Alibi" and "Ganymede."

"The Alibi" is the story of a homicidal personality. Middle-aged, married, and bored with the routine of his life, James Fenton feels that he has become a puppet, constrained by social customs and manners. Then, one day, he suddenly becomes aware of a sense of power within himself: "His was the master-hand that set the puppets jiggling" (11). He looks at the quiet, apathetic houses along the street and begins to express his new-found power in psychopathic terms: "They don't know, those people inside, how one gesture of mine, now, at this minute, might alter their world. A knock on the door, and someone answers—a woman yawning, an old man in carpet slippers, a child sent by its parents in irritation; and according to what I will, what I decide, their whole future will be decided. Faces smashed in. Sudden murder. Theft. Fire. It was as simple as that" (11–12).

Pretending he is an artist, Fenton rents a basement room in a run-down section of the city, "the air of poverty and decay" presenting "a contrast to the houses in his own small Regency square" (12). As in Victorian pornography, the victim of the upper-class manipulator is the lower-class woman. The only tenants in this slum dwelling are an Austrian woman named Anna Kaufman and her young boy Johnnie. Fenton plans to murder them both, believing that this act will demonstrate both his power and freedom as a human being.

Spending several hours in these lodgings each day (he tells his wife that he is working late at the office), Fenton becomes intensely interested in his paintings, first done as part of his charade but later taken seriously. Meanwhile, Anna has become very dependent upon him for companionship and money, and, when he says that he is going to take another apartment where he hopes to finish up his series of paintings, she becomes morose. He gathers up his materials and is about to leave when she asks him if he would throw away a package that she gives him. A policeman sees him drop the package into a trashcan and shows up at his home later to arrest him for disposing of a dead fetus.

Fenton confesses to the police and to his wife that indeed he was keeping this apartment where he painted nearly every day but that his relationship with Anna was an innocent one, all of which is true. When the police take him to the lodgings he discovers that Anna has turned on the gas and killed herself and Johnnie. Both the police and his wife believe that he murdered them, and Fenton, in an act of ironic despair, cries out, "All right, I'll confess everything. I was her lover, of course, and the child was mine. I turned on the gas this evening before I left the house. I killed them all" (49). The story ends with Fenton's false confession, a confession to a crime he had committed only in his imagination. His fantasy of power and freedom thus brings about his destruction.

Fenton's dissatisfaction with the routines and customs of middle-class life proves to be his undoing. Although the focus of this story is upon the melodrama of potential murder, its structure argues for the acceptance of conventional values. If one ventures out to become a sort of Nietzschean superman, imposing his own will upon events and becoming a law unto himself, then he is destroyed. In this case, the hero plants the seeds of self-destruction by merely fantasizing his plan for gratuitous murder. Of course, if one is a writer, like du Maurier, she may commit fictional murders with impunity and still retain her firm belief in the conventional manners and customs that hold her world so firmly together.

Influenced by Thomas Mann's "Death in Venice," du Maurier constructs a very compelling story in "Ganymede." The narrator is a classics scholar from England on holiday in Venice. Fired from his teaching position for "unsavoury practices," this sad and rather lonely man falls in love with a handsome young Italian waiter whom he christens "Ganymede." The middle-aged scholar imagines himself as

Zeus being served by this young cupbearer, and the fantasy provides him intense happiness during his stay in the hotel. Before long, however, he becomes involved with the boy's family and promises to get the young man a good-paying job in England. It becomes clear that there is a great gap between the scholar's and the boy's interests. The narrator considered giving him his prized collection of Shakespeare's plays but decides not to when he discovers that the boy really would like to have an Elvis Presley record. Their relationship develops, and the scholar's fantasy continues to grow when suddenly tragedy brings his homosexual dream to an end. While the boy is water-skiing, the narrator mishandles the tow line, and the boy is dragged under the propeller of the boat and killed. The narrator pays for all of the funeral expenses, and his life, as he says, "has become rather different" (126). With no living relative except his sister, whom he sees occasionally, he is once again facing the void. He concludes his tale by announcing that he has a little present for the fifteen-year-old boy training to be a waiter. He bought him a Perry Como record.

Du Maurier seems to be at her best in her more commonplace tales, such as this one and *The Parasites,* where she is not seeking melodramatic or supernatural effects. Like the Reverend Davey, the narrator is one of her "freaks," a social outcast who attempts to manipulate other people to satisfy his loneliness and unhappiness. Like Davey, who pays homage to the Druidical gods, Fenton identifies himself with the Greek god, Zeus. He is a sympathetic character until the end of the story where we learn that he is about to engage another young boy for his pleasure. Du Maurier's choice of first-person point of view is especially effective here, since it disallows any judgmental statements by an omniscient narrator. As far as the scholar is concerned, he is living a normal life, unwittingly revealing his selfishness, his pitiful loneliness, and his corruption. Above all else, he is guilty of hubris, an arrogant pride bred from sexual passion. When he first sees his "Ganymede" he remarks: "I myself was above him, did not exist in his time; and this self who was non-existent knew with every nerve fibre, every brain cell, every blood corpuscle that he was indeed Zeus, the giver of life and death, the immortal one, the lover; and that the boy who came towards him was his own beloved, his cup-bearer, his slave, his Ganymede" (95). Having inadvertently brought about the death of his first cupbearer, this would-be-Zeus descends from his classical heaven to the lowly world again, with a

Perry Como record under his arm, to seduce his next young boy. Du Maurier's grotesque sense of humor here is brilliant.

It often happens that a novel or short story is overshadowed by the film upon which it is based. *Gone with the Wind, The Wizard of Oz,* and *Rebecca* are cases in point. "Don't Look Now," the first story in *Not After Midnight,* may not be as well known as *Rebecca* but Nicholas Roeg's translation of the tale into film is one of the happiest marriages between fiction and film in recent years.

Du Maurier opens her story with a compellingly suspenseful sentence: " 'Don't look now,' John said to his wife, 'but there are a couple of old girls two tables away who are trying to hypnotise me.' "[7] John and Laura, an English couple, are on vacation in Venice in an attempt to distract themselves from the memory of the recent death of their young daughter, Christine, who died of meningitis. The two women sitting in the restaurant behind them are identical twins, only one of them is blind. They are wearing mannish clothes, and John jokingly speculates that they are lesbians or male twins in drag or hermaphrodites. Laura goes to the restroom, and when she returns she tells John that the blind twin told her that she saw their daughter Christine sitting between them and that she was laughing. Laura learned that one sister is a retired doctor from Edinburgh and that the other one has studied the occult all her life and was very psychic. "It's only since going blind," she tells John, "that she has really seen things, like a medium" (15).

John is an unbeliever, but upon seeing the blind sister's sightless eyes fixed upon him, "He felt himself held, unable to move, and an impending sense of doom, of tragedy, came upon him. His whole being sagged, as it were, in apathy, and he thought, 'This is the end, there is no escape, no future' " (16). These thoughts prove to be prophetic. A believer in such psychic forces as precognition and spirit communication, du Maurier allows the Tiresias-like sister to set the stage for the psychic drama to follow.

While John and Laura later roam through the back alleys of Venice in search of a restaurant they hear a scream. John catches a fleeting glimpse of a small figure that suddenly creeps from a cellar entrance below one of the houses opposite him and jumps into a boat below. "It was a child," he tells Laura, "a little girl—she couldn't have been more than five or six—wearing a short coat over her minute skirt, a pixie hood covering her head" (22).

When they get to the restaurant they run into the twin sisters again. This time the blind woman tells Laura that Christine is trying to tell their parents that they are in danger in Venice, that they should leave as soon as possible. Laura reports the warning to John and adds, "the extraordinary thing is that the blind sister says you're psychic and don't know it. You are somehow *en rapport* with the unknown, and I'm not" (27). John, as it turns out, is indeed psychic, and his refusal to believe in the supernatural eventually leads to his death.

A telephone call from London informs John and Laura that their son, Johnnie, is ill. Laura leaves Venice on a boat to catch a plane back home, and John is supposed to drive home the next day. John boards a ferry to fetch his car, and when another ferry passes him he thinks he sees Laura on it: "Laura, in her scarlet coat, the twin sisters by her side, the active sister with her hand on Laura's arm, talking earnestly, and Laura herself, her hair blowing in the wind, gesticulating, on her face a look of distress" (34). John returns to his hotel to wait for her, but when she fails to show up he tries to track down the sisters. When he checks at the restaurant, the proprietor informs him of a murderer at large: "A grizzly business. One woman found with her throat slit last week—a tourist too—and some old chap discovered with the same sort of knife wound this morning. They seem to think it must be a maniac, because there doesn't seem to be any motive" (42).

John reports his missing wife to the police, but soon afterwards he receives a call from London informing him that his son's appendicitis operation was successful and that his wife would like to speak to him. John has no explanation for his vision earlier in the day: "The point was he *had* seen all three of them on the vaporetto. It was not another woman in a red coat. The women *had* been there, with Laura. So what was the explanation? That he was going off his head? Or something more sinister?" (47). He tries desperately to convince himself that the whole business was a mistake, an hallucination. What he is unable to recognize at this point is that his vision is perfectly clear, only what he saw was a scene in the immediate future, namely that of Laura and the two sisters riding the ferry to his funeral.

John talks to the blind sister, and she explains that he had looked into the future but he naturally refuses to credit that explanation. He then proceeds to walk along the back alleys and suddenly sees the little girl with the pixie hood again "running as if her life depended upon it. . . . She was sobbing as she ran, not the ordinary cry of a frightened child, but the panic-stricken intake of breath of a helpless being in despair" (56, 57). He hears someone pursuing her and, thinking that they are both in danger of the homicidal maniac, he follows the child up the stairs within a courtyard and into a room leading off a small landing. He slams the door shut and bolts it, unwittingly sealing his fate: "The child struggled to her feet and stood before him, the pixie-hood falling from her head on to the floor. He stared at her, incredulity turning to horror, to fear. It was not a child at all but a little thick-set woman dwarf, about three feet high, with a great square adult head too big for her body, grey locks hanging shoulder-length, and she wasn't sobbing anymore, she was grinning at him, nodding her head up and down" (58).

He hears the police banging on the door. Suddenly the details of the past few days come together to form a horrifyingly clear picture: the figure he mistook for a child is the psychopathic killer, the blind sister was correct in the warning she conveyed to him through his dead daughter—his life was in danger, and the vision he had of the twin sisters with Laura was in fact an image of the future, as they will now proceed in such fashion to his funeral.

The dwarf withdraws a knife from her sleeve and hurls it at him with hideous strength piercing his throat. The creature begins gibbering in the corner, the police continue hammering on the door, and the sounds gradually grow fainter for him as he thinks, "Oh, God, what a bloody silly way to die" (57).

The gothic setting of a decaying Venice, the mad dwarf, the recurring glimpses into the future, the suspense, and the violence all go to make up an exciting story. Characteristically, du Maurier does not develop her characters to the point where we can have any strong feelings of sympathy for them. Instead, we watch with curiosity what *happens* to them. Life in a du Maurier tale is not so much depth of feeling as it is a sequence of events that eventually spell out the characters' fates. On a psychological level there is a suggestion here that John feels guilty for the death of his daughter, a feeling that makes him sensitive to the distress of the creature in the pixie hood, but du Maurier seems more concerned with his precognition than with his memories and how they affect his future.

The film *Don't Look Now* appeared in 1973, directed by Nicholas Roeg and starring Donald Sutherland as John, Julie Christie as Laura, Hilary Mason as the blind sister, and Clelia Matania as the other sister. In the picture John is an architect. After Christine accidentally drowns, the bereaved parents leave England and go to Venice, where John works at repairing the statuary and mosaics of a church.

Roeg uses the imagery of the film to draw events together. Christine, for example, is wearing a red slicker when she drowns. The malicious dwarf is also wearing a red slicker, making John's concern for her safety more compelling. When the film opens John is examining a slide of a church interior, and the top of the dwarf's red hood shows over one of the benches towards the rear of the church. A bleeding-red stain appears across the slide shortly before John has a premonition that something is wrong. He runs outside and sees the body of his daughter floating in the pond.

Another image is established at the opening of the film. Christine is riding her bicycle, and the camera focuses upon the front wheel going over a pane of glass, shattering it. When John is stabbed at the end of the film, all of the imagery comes together in his mind. He sees Laura and the sisters on the funeral boat, the bleeding stains across the slide, and in his death agony he kicks out a pane of glass with his foot. The sights and sounds associated with Christine's death close in upon him as his blood pumps from the large wound in his neck staining the floor.

Roeg also develops a nice contrast between pagan and Christian imagery in the film, something only vaguely hinted at in du Maurier's story. In Catholic Venice John earns his livelihood restoring the Christian images. Though we do not get the impression that either he or Laura are devout Christians, there is a scene in which Laura lights a votive candle for Christine. Set against the traditional Catholic images are those of a pagan world: the blind seer (Tiresias), the séance, and the malignant dwarf of folklore.

All of these images are timeless, floating between and connecting future, present, and past. The long scene of John and Laura's lovemaking is also consistent with the premonitory theme of the film. Throughout their passionate interlude there are frequent images of their getting dressed—flash-forwards. Pauline Kael observes that this scene "relates to the way eroticism is displaced throughout; dressing is splintered and sensualized, like fear and death—death most of all, with splashes of red." The film itself, she contends, is a mosaic of premonitions, and the dislocations are eroticized: "rotting Venice, the labyrinthine city of pleasure, with its crumbling, leering gargoyles, is obscurely, frighteningly sensual."[8]

Du Maurier's cool indifference to her characters, her clinical observation of their movements through the fate she has predestined for them, allows Roeg to flesh out this tale with a rich elegance and sensuality to create what Kael calls a "Borgesian setting—the ruins tokens of a mysteriously indifferent universe. . . . the romanticism isn't of the traditional Gothic variety but a coolly enigmatic sexiness."[9] Things are not what they seem in this dislocated world. A child in a red raincoat becomes a murderer. John's pursuit of the image of his daughter leads to his death, which is ironical in that her spirit warned him to leave Venice. The weird sisters—reminiscent of the ancient fates—are sometimes seen snickering together. Are they charlatans or seers? The erotic is not found in bed but in dressing and in the sinister streets of a deserted Venice and in the upper room in which John is alone with the grotesque dwarf. In short, Roeg turns du Maurier's gothic thriller into an erotic nightmare. As Kael says, "the picture is the fanciest, most carefully assembled Gothic enigma yet put on the screen."[10]

"A Border-Line Case" is a curious story of romantic incest. The narrator is a young actress named Shelagh Money. She attempts to amuse her ailing father by showing him some photographs from the family album. She will soon play the role of Cesario in *Twelfth Night* and pushes her hair behind her head to ape the character. Upon seeing this, her father suddenly stares at her with a look of horror and disbelief on his face and then dies. The tale then takes on the character of a detective story as Shelagh attempts to discover why her assumed appearance triggered her father's death.

After considerable digging for information, Shelagh tracks down her father's old friend, Nick Barry. Despite the fact that he is an older man, she falls in love with him and discovers that he is an Irish sympathizer who has organized a terrorist group in an attempt to unify Ireland. She soon enjoys a sexual interlude with him in the back of a grocery truck as he and his men head towards a terrorist attack on the border of Northern Ireland.

More probing leads to an amazing discovery. Nick was once ungraciously received by her mother and to seek revenge he "had a rough-and-tumble with her on the sofa" (162). Knowing all of this, Shelagh comments: "He's deceived my father, deceived my mother (serves her right), deceived the England he fought for for so many years, tarnished the uniform he wore, degraded his rank, spends his time now, and has done so for the past twenty years, trying to split this country wider apart than ever" (162–63). His reckless, adventuresome spirit, however, overwhelms her, and she confesses she loves him and is willing to throw over her theatrical career in order to "come and throw bombs with you" (163).

She returns to London and to the stage and soon receives a letter from Nick informing her that he is going to America to work on a book. He encloses a photograph of himself with a note written across the back: "Nick Barry as Cesario in *Twelfth Night*" (171). She realizes then that Nick is her father and that her presumed father, upon seeing her in a similar pose, had awakened "from a dream that had lasted twenty years. Dying, he discovered truth" (171). The story ends with Shelagh planning to leave the theater in order to dedicate herself to a life as a terrorist, "for only by hating can you purge away love, only by sword, by fire" (171).

The chief interest in this preposterous story is the oedipal feelings of the narrator. Incest comes into play here as Shelagh enjoys a sexual encounter with her father during a dangerous trip to the Irish border. The likelihood of being caught or killed adds to the thrill of the relationship. Shelagh does not at the time realize that the older man is her father. Her pleasure lies in being sexually dominated by a person long associated with her parent. When she discovers that Nick is indeed her father, she expresses no feelings of guilt or anguish but rather a strong determination to follow in his radical, violent ways. The adolescent and shrill tone of the story makes it unbelievable. It is compelling only as a youthful female fantasy of a sexually frustrated young woman.

"The Way of the Cross" is an entertaining account of an ill-sorted group of English pilgrims in Jerusalem. After the vicar of Little Bletford succumbs to an attack of influenza, the Reverend Edward Babcock is assigned the task of guiding the interesting group of tourists around the holy city. Lady Althea Mason, the most prominent of the party, is a vain, stuffy, wealthy woman whose mind is preoccupied with her looks and with social status. Her husband is a retired army colonel who sees everything from the military perspective of the 1940s. Jim Forster is the managing director of an up-and-coming plastics firm. A lecher, he later seduces Jill Smith, a young woman on her honeymoon. His wife, Kate Forster, expresses concern mainly for such topics as world poverty and starvation. Bob Smith and his bride, Jill, are attempting to come to terms with their new relationship. Miss Dean is a seventy-year-old spinster, perhaps the only mem-

ber of the group actually interested in the historical tour. She is
strongly attached to the vicar of Little Bletford, and Reverend Babcock's sudden replacement of her pastor spoils her idyll. Robin is the
nine-year-old grandson of the Masons. Reminiscent of Browning's
Pippa (in *Pippa Passes*), he is free, outspoken, intelligent, precocious,
and unaffected by the mad constraints of those around him.

Colonel Mason comes to realize during the tour that the military
has consumed his entire life. He tells Babcock that he would have
been given command of his regiment but that he had to leave the
army due to Althea's illness. Robin reports this conversation to Althea, who is overcome by doubt, guilt, and bewilderment. She had
always thought that her husband was content in his garden and in
arranging his military papers and books in the library.

Althea's complacency is further shocked when she loses the caps
from her front teeth after biting into a piece of hard bread. She looks
into a mirror: "The woman who stared back at her had two small filed
pegs stuck in her upper gums where the teeth should have been. They
looked like broken matchsticks, discoloured, black. All trace of
beauty had gone. She might have been some peasant who, old before
her time, stood begging at a street corner" (216).

Jill Smith, who had allowed Jim Foster to make love to her the
previous day, begins to feel guilty for deceiving her husband during
their honeymoon, especially since they are in the Holy Land. Jim,
meanwhile, gets caught up in a mob when he is chased by the police
for refusing to pay for a cheap medallion from a street merchant. Miss
Dean wanders off to the Pool of Bethesda to gather some of its mirac-
ulous waters into a vial. She plans to bring the water back to the vicar
in hopes of winning his continued approval. She slips on a damp
stone, however, falls into the pool and almost drowns in the holy
water. Even the Reverend Babcock manages to humiliate himself
when, at the Chapel of Golgotha, he has an attack of diarrhea from
some bad chicken he ate and passes out and fouls himself lying on the
church floor. Like Jonathan Swift, du Maurier takes especial delight
in focusing upon the repulsiveness of the human body (the description
of Lady Althea's mouth) and upon fecal humor.

In the last scene we see most of the principals sitting together,
physically or emotionally changed from what they were twenty-four
hours earlier. Miss Dean sits silently with a blanket over her knees.
Lady Althea is also silent, a chiffon scarf masking the lower part of
her face. She, too, has a blanket over her knees, and the Colonel holds

her hand beneath it. The Smiths more openly hold hands. The Forsters sit on either side of Miss Dean, and Reverend Babcock, in a
change of clothes, sits next to Robin. The story ends with Robin saying that he wishes he could have stayed two more days. Babcock asks
why and Robin replies, "Well, you never know. Of course it's not
very probable in this day and age, but we might have seen the Resurrection" (240).

The central theme of this story is that one must know the truth
before he or she can be free. A Jewish workman tells Robin that tomorrow is the Feast of the Unleavened Bread, "the Festival of our
Freedom," and that "everyone, everywhere, wanted freedom from
something" (238–39). Babcock learns humility; the Forsters are separated; the Masons are closer together; and Miss Dean is chastened.

Unlike most of du Maurier's short stories, which are terribly earnest and usually dependent upon the supernatural for their effect, this
one is remarkably simple. The light, mocking tone of the narrator,
the quickly but deftly drawn characters, and the clever setting that
contrasts their personal concerns with great moments in Christianity
give this tale a charm and cogency lacking in her other stories.

Although *The Rendezvous and Other Stories* was published in 1980,
all of the stories were written between 1930 and 1950. Why du
Maurier chose to resurrect them is not clear, for they clearly do not
further her reputation as a writer. Only her most die-hard fans, with
minds clouded by her past success, could celebrate the publication of
this collection. Paul Ableman, a reviewer for the *Spectator,* cleverly reviews this book by constructing an inner debate between his sentimental and rational mind. The rational mind, which prevails in the
end, offers some of the following damning observations: the characters
in the stories are wooden and unconvincing; the plots creak and depend upon outrageous coincidence; the prose is sloppy and chaotic
"and the whole volume hardly contains a shapely sentence"; the dialogue consists of "rent-a-line prefabricated units"; there is an absence
of "exact observation, authority over language, convincing motivation, significant plot or, to be brief, any evidence whatsoever of true
literary ability."[11]

"The Rendezvous" is one of the better stories in this volume. Robert Scrivener, a well-known English novelist, lives a lonely life until
he begins corresponding with a young woman from Geneva named
Annette Limoges. She flatters him in her letters, and soon the author
becomes infatuated with his unseen correspondent. Scheduled to give

a lecture in Geneva, he arranges to meet Annette there. He is dazzled by her beauty and longs to make love to her. It turns out, however, that she has fallen in love with a local bathing attendant named Alberto, a handsome fellow half Scrivener's age. Desperate to declare his love for her but too proud to be rejected in favor of the youth, Scrivener goes along with their joyful company, even to the point of tolerating their making love in his room when he is away from the hotel. He comes to the realization that his fame may win a beautiful young woman's attention but that it cannot compete with the sexual attraction of a younger man.

There are some interesting aspects of this story that suggest that du Maurier is constructing a rationalization and a defense for the sort of popular fiction she writes. One of Scrivener's friends, a popular novelist whose works sell in "ridiculous numbers," implies that Scrivener is "a fake, without the wide experience of life that his novels appeared to possess"[12] because he has never been married or had a lover. Scrivener is an elitist, careful to praise books that are unlikely to sell but that show some constructive approach to world problems. He "did not permit himself to be spoilt by his success, and he was careful to tell his friends that he would never be tempted by offers from Hollywood to prostitute his work upon the screen. As a matter of fact, no such offers came, but this was beside the point" (110–11). Obviously believing that she herself has had a wide experience of life, du Maurier uses Scrivener as an example of the limited literary purist, a strawman to be devastated by his private needs, which, ironically, are depicted in a Hollywood motion picture.

After his lecture in Geneva Scrivener receives a note from Annette telling him that she and Alberto will be using his apartment that evening. In despair, Scrivener goes to a theater where he sees a movie about a middle-aged man whose life turns sour and who murders his wife and falls in love with his step-daughter. Identifying with the hero, Scrivener weeps uncontrollably and sees the works he has written as lost to him "across the wasted years of his own dull, empty life" (137). When the film credits are run he suddenly realizes that the picture was based upon his writer friend's best-selling novel that he had always despised.

The autobiographical fable embedded within this tale, then, argues that du Maurier's wide experience, her best-selling novels, and her concessions to Hollywood are all meritorious. The elitist writers may have the adulation of the snobbish literary establishment but real life moves on a lower, more powerful plane, and the elitist will one day come to realize that.

In most of her short fiction du Maurier is primarily interested in conclusions and in the events that lead to those conclusions. Character, atmosphere, language, social commentary—all are of secondary interest to her as she plunges her undefined characters into a sequence of events that inextricably lead them to a predestined, usually surprising, fate. Her stories present life in neat, tidy little packages. Her characters are manipulated by their contrived future, their every gesture and word leading to a preconceived conclusion. Du Maurier's best stories avoid this easy pattern in favor of a more complex, ambiguous view of life. "The Birds," "Don't Look Now," "The Way of the Cross," and "Ganymede" are four of her most convincing and entertaining stories. Like *Rebecca* and *The Parasites,* two of her best novels, they convey a cogent sense of the terror and comedy of ordinary human life.

Chapter Seven
Conclusion

In many ways Daphne du Maurier's life resembles a fairy tale. Born into a family with a rich artistic and historical background, the daughter of a famous actor, she was indulged as a child and grew up enjoying enormous freedom from financial and parental restraint. She never held a job; rather, she spent her youth sailing boats, traveling with her friends, and writing stories. A prestigious publishing house accepted her first novel when she was in her young twenties. Its publications brought her not only fame but a handsome military prince who married her. Her subsequent novels became best-sellers, earning her enormous wealth and fame. Alfred Hitchcock's films based on her novels proceeded to make her one of the best-known authors in the world. She began to live like a fairy princess in a mansion called Menabilly, and the books she wrote there during the next two decades sold millions of copies throughout the world.

Although she endured moments of loneliness and anxiety during the war years, du Maurier clearly was not a struggling artist who had to suffer years of rejection and criticism before achieving success. She has lived a charmed and genteel life, insulated from the disturbing issues of her day. Her contemporaries were dealing in their fiction with themes related to the war, alienation, religion, Marxism, psychology, poverty, and art. Many were experimenting with new techniques, such as stream of consciousness and the use of multiple personae. Du Maurier, on the other hand, continued to write "old-fashioned" novels with straightforward narratives that appealed to a conventional audience's love of fantasy, adventure, sexuality, and mystery. At an early age she recognized that her principal readership was comprised of women, and she cultivated their loyal readership through several decades by embodying their desires and dreams in her novels and short stories.

Du Maurier's literary style seems inextricably related to her insulated life-style. There is a vast body of knowledge and a large segment of society she never really knew or understood. *Hungry Hill*, for example, is a notable failure because she knows little about Ireland and even less about the Irish poor. She is not interested in ideas, in science, technology, religion, politics, economics, or philosophy. She exhibits little curiosity about or knowledge of cultures other than her own. Her circumscribed world is a fantasy built upon Cornish history, family life, sailing, nineteenth-century poetry, gardens, love affairs, upper-middle-class sensibilities, and supernatural happenings. Her fiction reflects the psychology of a reclusive woman accustomed to success who, in her youth, was desirous of burning with a hard gemlike flame, aspiring towards freedom and heightened emotion, and who, later in life, was content to stoke the home fires of family and patriotism.

The literary establishment clearly wants nothing to do with Daphne du Maurier. There are no critical essays or books about her. Her only critics to date have been the many book reviewers who, for the most part, heralded each novel as a gift of genius, though most agree that she never surpassed the level of excellence she achieved in *Rebecca*. The fact that millions of people read her novels certainly works against her approval by literary critics, who are not inclined to prize what the popular audience does. By the standards of contemporary literary criticism, most of du Maurier's works do not hold up well. Her prose, while straightforward and clear, is not especially interesting. There is little imagery, symbolism, or ambiguity in her writing. Her characters are often undeveloped, and her plots become all-important. Her style is conventional, her sentences unmemorable, and her story lines contrived. Compared with authors like Graham Greene or John Steinbeck she seems shallow and commercial.

Why, then, have her novels been so successful? Why is it that she has so many closet readers, sophisticated people who enjoy her works but who are reluctant to proclaim their enjoyment? Despite her failure as a thinker and as a stylist, du Maurier is a master storyteller who knows how to manipulate female fantasies. She creates a world that is simple, romantic, usually unambiguous, adventuresome, mysterious, dangerous, erotic, picturesque, and satisfying. It is a world that contrasts sharply with the mundane realities of ordinary existence, and it is a world that does not require the reader to suffer the pains of introspection and analysis. It is, in short, a world that brings considerable pleasure to millions of readers, especially women.

Three of her novels, however, transcend the narcotic effect of the body of her work: *The Progress of Julius, Rebecca,* and *The Parasites.* In these three works, du Maurier exhibits a powerful psychological realism reflecting her intense feelings about her father and, to a lesser degree, about her mother. The vision that underlies these novels is that of an author overwhelmed by her obsession with her father's sexual and authoritarian presence. This vision lends the stories a special vitality. Furthermore, the style of these novels stands out from that of the others in its relative simplicity, in its heightened attention to small detail, and in its depiction of unspectacular characters and events. A novel like *Frenchman's Creek,* for example, depends upon extravagant action, a broad land and seascape, and fairy-tale characters, while *The Parasites* works within the small compass of a living room within a twenty-four-hour period and focuses upon a neurotic but believable family. The love between Dona and her French pirate has no substance: it is a fairy tale, a projected fantasy. The incestuous feelings between Niall and Maria, on the other hand, vibrate with genuine emotion and are rooted in the particulars of their unusual past. Similarly, the narrator's involvement with both Maxim de Winter and Mrs. Danvers sweeps the reader into the midst of the triangle. Even the melodramatic murder of Gabriel Lévy in *The Progress of Julius,* through its oedipal significance, has a powerful psychological impact on the reader. The feelings in these works are believable and dynamic, as if conjured up from the depths of the human psyche. In these three novels, du Maurier manages to create a compelling vision of human character that transcends melodrama, creaky plots, and contrived endings.

Rebecca, "The Birds," and "Don't Look Now" also stand out among her works as landmarks in the development of the modern gothic tale. Du Maurier has breathed new life into the old forms of the gothic novel to come up with a classic tale of the Other Woman. Millions of women have identified with the plain, nameless narrator of *Rebecca,* a woman who defines her personality by overcoming the mother figure of Rebecca to win the lasting love of her father-lover. "The Birds" and "Don't Look Now" establish the twentieth-century sense of dislocation. The accepted order of things suddenly and for no apparent reason is upset. The great chain of being breaks, and people find themselves battling for their lives against creatures they always assumed inferior to themselves: birds and children. The continuity of time itself is in question in "Don't Look Now" as the future bleeds into the present.

Perhaps du Maurier wrote too much, catered too cynically to the popular taste of her audience, but she created the "classic" gothic novel of the twentieth century, setting the stage for hundreds of imitators grinding out formulaic tales in the Harlequin Romance series and others. Du Maurier has done her fair share of grinding out stories as well, but she has the talent to rise to the surface of literary respectability that many of her followers lack. The unseen Rebecca, Mrs. Danvers, and Manderley itself have become etched indelibly upon the imaginations of millions of people who have read *Rebecca* or have seen the motion picture. If Daphne du Maurier had written only *Rebecca*, she would still be one of the great shapers of popular culture and the modern imagination. Few writers have created more magical and mysterious places than Jamaica Inn and Manderley, buildings invested with a rich and brooding character that gives them a memorable life of their own. Although du Maurier does not subscribe to a conventional religious belief, she transformed the places she inhabited or visited—such as Ferryside, Jamaica Inn, and Menabilly—into gothic paradises, sacred structures of her imagination. Perhaps the passage in the Bible that best summarizes both her obsession with her father and her religious sense of place is that of St. John: "In my Father's house there are many mansions. . . . I go to prepare a place for you."

Notes and References

Chapter One

1. For a fuller account of the du Maurier family, see Leonée Ormond, *George du Maurier* (Pittsburgh: University of Pittsburgh Press, 1969), and Richard Kelly, *George du Maurier* (Boston: Twayne, 1983).
2. *Gerald: A Portrait* (London, 1934), 85; hereafter cited as *Gerald*.
3. *Growing Pains* (London, 1977), 27; hereafter cited as *GP*.
4. *The Rebecca Notebook and Other Memories* (New York, 1980), 240; hereafter cited as *RN*.
5. "Menabilly," *House and Garden* 92 (August 1947); 114.
6. "Faces to the Sun," *Good Housekeeping* 112 (April 1941); 19.
7. Ibid.
8. Ibid.
9. "Menabilly," 114.
10. Ibid.
11. Ibid., 118.
12. Ibid.
13. Harrison Smith, *Saturday Review of Literature* 24 (29 November 1941); 3, 17–18.
14. Quoted in *Publishers' Weekly* 153 (31 January 1948); 632.
15. Beverly Nichols, *Ladies Home Journal* 73 (November 1956); 25.
16. Ibid.
17. Ibid., 27, 31.
18. Ibid., 27, 32.

Chapter Two

1. H. C. Harwood, "New Novels," *Saturday Review* 151 (28 February 1931); 311.
2. *The Loving Spirit* (London, 1931), 3; page numbers hereafter cited in text.
3. *Growing Pains*, 119.
4. *The Rebecca Notebook and Other Memories*, 268; hereafter cited as *RN*.
5. Geoffrey Terwilliger, "The Reality of Wishes," *New York Herald Tribune*, 2 August 1931, 5.
6. Ibid.
7. *Spectator* 146 (28 February 1931); 320.
8. Harwood, *Saturday Review*, 311.

9. *I'll Never Be Young Again* (London, 1932), 13; page numbers hereafter cited in text.

10. *Punch,* 182 (29 June 1932); 725.

11. Lisle Bell, "Portrait of a Volcanic Egotist," *New York Herald Tribune Review of Books,* 27 August 1933, 6.

12. *The Progress of Julius* (London, 1933), 25; page numbers hereafter cited in text.

13. Graham Greene, "Fiction," *Spectator* 150 (7 April 1933); 508.

14. Elmer Davis, "Avarice at Large," *Saturday Review of Literature* 10 (19 August 1933); 54.

15. Anne Armstrong, "New Novels," *Saturday Review* 155 (1 April 1933); 316.

16. *Punch* 184 (12 April 1933); 420.

17. Greene, *Spectator,* 508.

18. *Jamaica Inn* (London, 1936), 9; page numbers hereafter cited in text.

19. "Romance in Cornwall," *Times Literary Supplement,* 11 January 1936; 33.

20. Sean O'Faolain, "New Novels," *Spectator* 156 (24 January 1936); 144.

21. Donald Spoto, *The Dark Side of Genius: The Life of Alfred Hitchcock* (Boston: Little Brown, 1983), 184.

22. Raymond Durgnat, "The Strange Case of Alfred Hitchcock—Part Six: Touch and Go," *Films and Filming* 16 (1970); 58.

Chapter Three

1. Kay Mussell, *Fantasy and Reconciliation* (Westport, Conn., 1984), 9.

2. *Rebecca* (London, 1938), 1; page numbers hereafter cited in text.

3. "No Sunnybrook Farm," *Time* 32 (24 October 1938); 70.

4. "Survival," *Times Literary Supplement,* 6 August 1938, 517.

5. V. S. Pritchett, "Daphne Du Maurier Writes a Victorian Thriller," *Christian Science Monitor,* 14 September 1938, 12.

6. Eleanor Godfrey, "The Second Wife," *Canadian Forum* 18 (October 1938); 218.

7. John Patton, "Exciting Modern Gothic Tale," *New York Herald Tribune,* 15 September 1938, 3.

8. *The Rebecca Notebook and Other Memories,* 3; hereafter cited as *RN.*

9. Spoto, *The Dark Side of Genius,* 184.

10. Ibid., 213.

11. Screenplay for *Rebecca.* Reproduction of studio-issued original script, dated 26 March 1940, 161.

12. Ibid., 163.

13. Ibid.

14. Ibid.

15. Richard Kiely, *The Romantic Novel in England* (Cambridge, Mass., 1972), 252.

16. Ibid.

17. Spoto, *The Dark Side of Genius,* 216.

18. Ibid., 219.

19. Otis Ferguson, "Slight Cases of Marriage," *New Republic* 102 (8 April 1940); 474.

20. Raymond Durgnat, "Missing Women," *Films and Filming* 16 (July 1970); 57.

21. Ibid., 58.

22. Ibid.

Chapter Four

1. John Cawelti, *Adventure, Mystery, and Romance* (Chicago, 1976), 41.

2. Ibid., 42.

3. James Agee, "Films," *Nation* 159 (14 October 1944); 443.

4. Ibid.

5. Ibid.

6. Ibid.

7. Robert Louis Stevenson, "A Gossip on Romance," *Memories and Portraits* (New York: Scribner's, 1900), 255.

8. *Frenchman's Creek* (London, 1941), 16; page numbers hereafter cited in text.

9. John Lardner, "It All Depends," *New Yorker* 20 (30 September 1944); 48.

10. "Pirates and Lovers," *Times Literary Supplement,* 13 September 1944, 457.

11. "New Picture," *Time* 44 (9 October 1944); 94.

12. Philip Hartung, "So-So," *Commonweal* 40 (13 October 1944); 614.

13. Agee, *Nation,* 443.

14. John McCarten, *New Yorker* 23 (18 October 1947); 105.

15. *The King's General* (London, 1946), 56; page numbers hereafter cited in text.

16. "Through Cromwell's Times with Flashlight and Pick," *New Yorker* 21 (12 January 1946); 78.

17. "The Matinee Idol," in *The Rebecca Notebook,* 241.

18. Ivor Brown, "When Mayfair and Bohemia Meet," *New York Times Book Review,* 1 January 1950, 1.

19. Ibid.

20. *The Parasites* (London, 1949), 9; page numbers hereafter cited in text.

21. *My Cousin Rachel* (London, 1951), 8; page numbers hereafter cited in text.

22. John Barkham, "And Surf Booming on the Beach," *New York Times Book Review*, 10 February 1952, 5.

23. Bosley Crowther, *New York Times*, 26 December 1952, 20.

24. *Mary Anne* (London, 1954), 20; page numbers hereafter cited in text.

25. *Growing Pains*, 26.

26. Geoffrey Bruun, "Out of the du Maurier Family Album: Lively Lady in a Man's World," *New York Herald Tribune Book Review*, 20 June 1954, 11.

27. *Catholic World* 179 (September 1954); 475.

Chapter Five

1. "This I Believe," in *The Rebecca Notebook*, 264.

2. *The Scapegoat* (London, 1957), 5; page numbers hereafter cited in text.

3. Anthony Boucher, "Another Man's Life," *New York Times Book Review*, 24 February 1957, 5, 26.

4. John Bayley, "New Novels," *Spectator* 198 (12 April 1957); 494.

5. *The Rebecca Notebook*, 265.

6. "Take Me Back to Manderley," *Time* 69 (25 February 1957); 102.

7. "Other Men's Shoes," *Times Literary Supplement*, 10 May 1957, 293.

8. Boucher, "Another Man's Life," *New York Times Book Review*, 5.

9. *"This I Believe,"* in *The Rebecca Notebook*, 265.

10. Howard Thompson, *New York Times Film Review*, 7 August 1959, 28.

11. *The Glass-Blowers* (London, 1963), 54; page numbers hereafter cited in text.

12. *The Rebecca Notebook*, 264.

13. Patricia MacManus, "Starting a Flap," *Book Week* 2 (11 July 1965); 18.

14. *New Yorker* 41 (17 July 1965); 108.

15. *The Flight of the Falcon* (London, 1965), 14; page numbers hereafter cited in text.

16. *The Rebecca Notebook*, 268.

17. Ibid., 269.

18. Ibid., 268.

19. *The House on the Strand* (London, 1969), 127; page numbers hereafter cited in text.

20. Edward Weeks, "The Peripatetic Reviewer," *Atlantic* 231 (February 1973); 101.

21. *Rule Britannia* (London, 1972), 14; page numbers hereafter cited in text.

22. *The Parasites,* 13.

23. "Romantics and Insiders," *Economist* 245 (11 November 1972); n.p.

24. Ibid.

25. Joseph Kanon, "Popcorn at Eight," *Saturday Review of Arts* 1 (January 1973); 85.

Chapter Six

1. *The Breaking Point* (London, 1952), 7.

2. *The Apple Tree* (London, 1952), 85; page numbers hereafter cited in text.

3. Spoto, *The Dark Side of Genius,* 454.

4. Brendan Gill, *New Yorker* 39 (6 April 1963); 177.

5. Gary Arnold, "Birds and Gulls," *Moviegoer* 1 (Winter 1964); 34.

6. *The Breaking Point,* 7; page numbers hereafter cited in text.

7. *Not After Midnight* (London, 1971), 9; page numbers hereafter cited in text.

8. Pauline Kael, "Labyrinths," *New Yorker* 49 (24 December 1973); 71, 68.

9. Ibid., 68.

10. Ibid., 71.

11. Paul Ableman, "The Intruder," *Spectator* 245 (15 November 1980); 20.

12. *The Rendezvous and Other Stories* (London, 1980), 115; page numbers hereafter cited in text.

Selected Bibliography

PRIMARY SOURCES

1. Books

The Loving Spirit. London: Heinemann, 1931.
I'll Never Be Young Again. London: Heinemann, 1932.
The Progress of Julius. London: Heinemann, 1933.
Gerald: A Portrait. London: Gollancz, 1934.
Jamaica Inn. London: Gollancz, 1936.
The du Mauriers. London: Gollancz, 1937.
Rebecca. London: Gollancz, 1938.
Frenchman's Creek. London: Gollancz, 1941.
Hungry Hill. London: Gollancz, 1943.
The Years Between. London: Gollancz, 1945.
The King's General. London: Gollancz, 1946.
September Tide. London: Gollancz, 1949.
The Parasites. London: Gollancz, 1949.
The Young George du Maurier: A Selection of His Letters, 1860–1867. (Editor.)
    London: Peter Davies, 1951.
My Cousin Rachel. London: Gollancz, 1951.
The Apple Tree. London: Gollancz, 1952.
Mary Anne. London: Gollancz, 1954.
The Scapegoat. London: Gollancz, 1957.
The Breaking Point. London: Gollancz, 1959.
The Infernal World of Branwell Bronte. London: Gollancz, 1960.
The Glass-Blowers. London: Gollancz, 1963.
The Flight of the Falcon. London: Gollancz, 1965.
Vanishing Cornwall. London: Gollancz, 1967.
The House on the Strand. London: Gollancz, 1969.
Not After Midnight. London: Gollancz, 1971.
Rule Britannia. London: Gollancz, 1972.
Golden Lads. London: Gollancz, 1975.
The Winding Stair. London: Gollancz, 1976.
Echoes from the Macabre. London: Gollancz, 1976.
Growing Pains. London: Gollancz, 1977.
The Rendezvous and Other Stories. London: Gollancz, 1980.
The Rebecca Notebook and Other Memories. New York: Doubleday, 1980; Lon-

don: Gollancz, 1981. (Omits some of the stories and essays in the American edition.)

2. Essays

"Faces to the Sun," *Good Housekeeping* 112 (April 1941); 19.

"Menabilly: The Most Beautiful House I Have Ever Seen," *House and Garden* 92 (August 1947); 92–97, 113, 114, 118.

"My Love Affair With Crete," *Holiday* 49 (March 1970–71); 68, 78–79.

"The Place Has Taken Hold of Me," *Saturday Evening Post* 249 (December 1977); 48–50.

SECONDARY SOURCES

Cawelti, John G. *Adventure, Mystery, and Romance.* Chicago: University of Chicago Press, 1976. A perceptive discussion of the formulas for popular novels such as the romance, adventure story, and the mystery.

Gilbert, Sandra. "Costumes of the Mind: Transvestism as Metaphor in Modern Lierature," *Critical Inquiry* 2 (Winter 1980); 391–417. Tedious but occasionally interesting discussion of the sexual significance of costume.

Kiely, Robert. *The Romantic Novel in England.* Cambridge, Mass.: Harvard University Press, 1972. A thorough analysis of the nature of the romantic novel of the eighteenth and nineteenth centuries.

————. *The Gothic Tradition in Fiction.* New York: Columbia University Press, 1979. A comprehensive study of the English gothic romance in the eighteenth and nineteenth century.

Modleski, Tania. *Loving with a Vengeance.* New York: Methuen, 1982. A study of mass-produced fantasies for women: Harlequin romances, gothic novels, and television soap operas.

Mussell, Kay. *Fantasy and Reconciliation.* Westport, Conn.: Greenwood Press, 1984. An excellent analysis of the contemporary formulas of women's romance fiction.

Sherwood, Robert E., and Joan Harrison, Screenplay for *Rebecca.* Reproduction of studio-issued original script, dated 26 March 1940, for the Hitchcock motion picture.

Stockwell, LaTourette. "Best Sellers and the Critics: A Case History," *College English* 16 (January 1955); 214–21. Perhaps the only article qua article written about du Maurier. A facile and patronizing attempt to explain du Maurier's great popularity among the masses and her failure to elicit notices from serious literary critics.

Index